KALEIDOSCOPE

LEICESTERSHIRE

Edited by Simon Harwin

First published in Great Britain in 1999 by
POETRY NOW YOUNG WRITERS
Remus House, Coltsfoot Drive,
Woodston,
Peterborough, PE2 9JX
Telephone (01733) 890066

HB ISBN 0 75430 664 X
SB ISBN 0 75430 665 8

FOREWORD

This year, the Poetry Now Young Writers' Kaleidoscope competition proudly presents the best poetic contributions from over 32,000 up-and-coming writers nationwide.

Successful in continuing our aim of promoting writing and creativity in children, each regional anthology displays the inventive and original writing talents of 11-18 year old poets. Imaginative, thoughtful, often humorous, *Kaleidoscope Leicestershire* provides a captivating insight into the issues and opinions important to today's young generation.

The task of editing inevitably proved challenging, but was nevertheless enjoyable thanks to the quality of entries received. The thought, effort and hard work put into each poem impressed and inspired us all. We hope you are as pleased as we are with the final result and that you continue to enjoy *Kaleidoscope Leicestershire* for years to come.

CONTENTS

Redmoor High School

        Amy Garner   100

The Rutland College

Trevor Bell	100
Zoë Berry	101
Emma Chivers	102
Sally Sturgess	103
Clare Connors	104
Lucy Riches	105
Paula Brown	105
Emma Keogh	106
Rachel Sam Veasey	106
Thom Wilson	107
Andrew Bewick	107
Laura Grey	108
Sandra Deal	108
Helen Roberts	109
Rebecca Potter	110
Adam Smith	111
James Waller	112
Hannah Taylor	112
Vicky Ellis	113
Kaye Houston	114
Laura Plant	115
Louisa Daniel	116
Melanie Finnemore	117
Deborah Glancy	118
Krystina Kinkade	118
Julia Riley	119
Laura Orton	120
Richard Chisholm	121
Alexa Kenny	122
Jonathan Bird	122
Emily Moss	123
Siân Penfold	124
Alan Lloyd	125
Kathryn Walters	126

The Poems

MY CRAZY RELATIONS

I have a chimpanzee, a very small chimpanzee.
She constantly runs around the house.
She eats a lot of sweets, and she is very kind.
I call her my cousin Christina.

I have a bear, a very cuddly bear.
She is always shopping.
She also drinks tea.
She is very soft, I call her Nan.

I have an ostrich, a very tall ostrich.
She is always very friendly and also kind.
She is very funny.
I call her my friend, Sophie.

I have a cheetah, a very big cheetah.
He runs far and very, very fast.
He eats great quantities of food.
I call him my cousin, Mike.

Lauren Canning (11)
Dixie Grammar School

A MYSTERY

Her hair, blonde and shiny,
her dress, green and sparkly,
her smile shows delight.
The place she is in has a wild atmosphere.
Her eyes show tiredness,
but still, they dazzle.

Jennie Anne Agnew (13)
Dixie Grammar School

FAMILY OF ANIMALS

I have a bear, a big, fuzzy bear,
He likes to be the biggest in the family.
He beats me at things that gets me annoyed.
I call him Dad.

I have a cat, a graceful cat,
That keeps me clean and feeds me well.
She seems very hard but really she is soft inside,
I call her Mum.

I have a chimp, who is a bit of a monkey,
He is always doing jobs,
He is rather busy.
I call him Grandpa.

There is a hyena,
Who is not quite there.
He runs very fast with plenty of energy.
That is me, the son.

Oliver Warner (11)
Dixie Grammar School

ELEPHANTS

Elephants walking in the sun.
Trunks are swinging from side to side.
Long, shiny, white, ivory tusks.
Big, grey bodies with wrinkled skin.
Huge feet pounding on the hard ground.
Searching for some shade or somewhere cool.

Sinking into mud to cool off
And sucking up water to spray.
Babies play and splash in the mud.
No one suspects a thing until . . .
Bang, bang! Echoes all around them.
An elephant lies dead in the mud.

Jessica Groves (12)
Dixie Grammar School

MY ANIMAL FAMILY

I have a gorilla,
He is big and fat.
He is quite strong.
I call him Dad.

We have a little kangaroo,
She jumps all over the place.
She always carries things in her pouch.
I think it is my mum.

I have a little doggy,
She always eats her tea.
She likes to have some biscuits.
I think it might be me.

I have a cheeky monkey,
He is mad.
He always runs and bangs his head,
He is my cousin, Paul.

I have a little 'sister',
She is quite mad.
She likes chasing frogs.
She is my dog.

Gemma Parkes (11)
Dixie Grammar School

THE ANIMAL HOUSE!

I have a bat, a very blind bat,
Who gets all the money for us.
He gets mad at me a lot.
He is out most of the day.
I call him Dad.

I also have a cat, a nice and cuddly cat.
She looks after the house and the horse.
She cares for her young.
She is always there.
I call her Mum.

I have a dog, a weird and wonderful dog.
Her head is brown.
She has a weird frown.
She coughs a lot.
I call her my sister.

Then there is me,
I know what I am,
I'm the black sheep.

Sean Smith (11)
Dixie Grammar School

THE SNAKE

I was walking one night
And had a big fright
And there before me was a snake.
It was scaly and long
And had a big tongue
And not a move did it make.

I stared at it long
But something was wrong
And it looked about to strike.
I stared some more
And I dropped to the floor
As I felt the poisonous bite.

William Beasley (11)
Dixie Grammar School

THE ANIMAL HOUSE

I have a hippo,
He's big, lazy and he eats a lot,
He lies around all day telling us what to do,
I call him Dad.

I have a swan,
She's busy from dawn till dusk,
She gets me everywhere on time,
And sees we have all we need,
I call her Mum.

I have a butterfly,
She was once slow and ate plenty,
But after going to sleep in her comfy sleeping bag,
She now flutters around all day and I hardly see her,
I call her Sister.

I am a magpie,
Or you'd think so to look at my room,
I never throw anything away,
But that's me.

Matthew Haynes (11)
Dixie Grammar School

ELEPHANTS

Swinging its long trunk,
Sliding in the wet mud.
Its body pattern covered in mud.
Sucking up water.
Baby elephants playing with their mothers.
Blazing trumpet sound,
Elephants from all over come stamping.
Bang!
Old elephant sank to its knees,
Stamping drifts away,
Old elephant's body lay still in the dirty water.

Kiran Chana (11)
Dixie Grammar School

BATTLE

The battle is raging
People are injured or dying
The spotlights are on searching
Searching for what?
There is nothing
It is dark, everything is dark
The shadows look funny
They play with us
Was that someone?
Or was it a shadow?

Laurence Hurst (12)
Dixie Grammar School

THE ANIMALS' PICNIC

Monkey munched a mango
Leema longed for lasagne
Parrots picked at the pineapple
Hyena hurled hot dogs
Snake sucked the sweets
Cheetah charged at the chocolate
Aardvark asked for an apple
Insects insisted on Indian food
Gorilla grabbed the grapes
Rats reached for the raisins
Jaguar jumped the jelly.

Ekraj Chana (12)
Dixie Grammar School

THE TROPICAL RAINFOREST

Plodding through the thick, oozing mud.
Observing the reaching trees and their seeping, spreading branches.
I am ecstatic seeing this lush, green hallway of beauty.
An iguana pads hungrily towards those succulent bush leaves.
Tropical plants standing out in this dark cavern, sheltered by the trees.
An enormous waterfall cascading into the vast splash pool.
It could all be destroyed by the tree-fellers grasping for money.
It is such a shame that we cannot have this environment
                              nearer to home where I can protect it.

Ben Gardner (12)
Dixie Grammar School

ORPHAN

Sitting lowly in a cardboard box
Shivering, hungry in the rain.
Nobody notices her
Sitting in the grey streets
Of the dark, dirty city.

Face is pale, skin is dirty.
Cold, shrivelled fingers
Grasping knees to body,
Trying vainly to keep warm.
Clothes resemble a sack,
Dirty and sparse.

Her empty eyes, the scars
On her face tell her past.
She starts to cry, the tears
Trickle down her skinny face and
Over her thin body.

She doesn't deserve this.
Nobody does.

Heather Powell (13)
Dixie Grammar School

MY FAMILY OF ANIMALS

I have a gorilla in my house,
Always keeping everyone under control.
He always eats his food in great amounts,
And I call him Dad.

I have a dove in my house.
She always does the housework,
Making sure everything is spick and span.
She makes dinner, I call her Mum.

I also have a kitten.
She is silly and playful,
And she is sometimes a pain,
But she is funny, I call her my sister.

Then there's me,
I know what I am!
I am a cheeky monkey.

Ben Doyle (11)
Dixie Grammar School

MY GREAT FAMILY

I have a cat in my house.
She's sweet and kind
and does everything to make me happy.
Her fur is red and brown.
I call her Mum.

I have a rabbit in my house.
He's fun to be with
and occasionally vicious.
Especially when I'm cheeky.
I call him Dad.

I have a hamster in my house.
He's vicious but funny
and very busy, running around in his world.
I call him Josh.

And well, you all know
Me!

Andrew Linforth (11)
Dixie Grammar School

NETWORK CONNECTIONS

Said computer 1 to computer 2
'Look I've got something new,
Now I can do something I couldn't do.'

Said computer 2 to computer 1
'It won't be much fun,
You'll always be on the run.'

Computer 1 said
'I'd sooner be dead,
Than not move ahead.'

Computer 2 lit up
'Ah ha, but what if you crack up,
You haven't any back up.'

Said the first computer
'But this will make me work faster,
I've got an on-line plaster.'

Said computer 2
'I don't like you,
You don't think things through.'

Computer 1 said to computer 2
'Gorble, garble, geeble, gobloo,
Garble, gorble, gleeble, gobloo.'

Said computer 2
'That's the end of you,
It's given you super virus 2!'

Robert Morgan (12)
Dixie Grammar School

MY MAD HOUSEHOLD

I have a bear,
a very big bear
with very little hair.
He sits in his chair
working with care.
I call him Dad.

I also have a mother hen,
she's cuddly and when,
her little chicks are naughty
she clucks and squawks and flaps her wings.
I call her Mum.

I have a big rabbit.
He is always eating.
The only strange thing is that
real rabbits eat salad and he does not.
I call him my brother.

Always jumping, always springing
never sitting still,
just like a grasshopper
that's my little bro.

In my house there is a bird of paradise.
She is beautiful and has learnt to cope
with anything and everything.
And, that is me!

Georgia Yates (11)
Dixie Grammar School

FAST FOODS

Pizza, chips and chocolate too,
Someone must like these, but who?
Children like all of these,
Grannies say 'Don't eat that, please.'

Burgers, fries and ice-cream,
These won't keep you lean,
Cookies, crisps and all that,
These will make you rather fat.

Grannies are old fashioned with veg and meat,
They really think you should sit down to eat,
Mums think fruit is good for you,
And milk and salad too.

I think a cream cake or sweets,
Most definitely beats,
An apple or a pear,
Or any fruit that's ever there.

I adore fast food,
Even if I'm in a mood,
It really is the very best
I arrive, McDonalds does the rest.

Laura Walker (12)
Dixie Grammar School

A DOLPHIN

To have a dolphin for a friend,
Is not a friend you'd like to lend.
He swims around,
Homeward bound.
And he always comes back to me!

He eats small fish,
Off my big round dish.
He would never bite,
His mouth is shut tight.
He always swims up to me!

Cathy Goodwin (12)
Dixie Grammar School

THE ANIMAL HOUSE

I have a lion, a furry faced lion,
He works very hard, all day long,
He loses his temper easily,
I call him my dad.

I have a cat, a very friendly cat,
She helps me all the time,
And looks after me,
She's my mum.

I have a bear, a quite big bear,
He often stays away from home,
And when I call him, he shouts at me.
He's my older brother.

I also have a panther, a big black panther,
He lives away from home.
He looks after people and is very gentle,
He's my oldest brother.

And then there's me,
I always run around and mess about.
I'm the little monster.

Priya Kambo (11)
Dixie Grammar School

FRANK!

My hamster,
He is a gangster!
He rummages all night
Then I turn on the light
He freezes, still and quiet.
I can't hear him anymore
So,

I turn off the light
I listen in vain
Then a fluffy, puffy fat thing
Starts rummaging again!

In the morning,
When I am yawning . . .
I hear the wheel go 'Clank!'
So I get out of bed and I say to myself,
'Why on earth do I have Frank?'

Ben Davies (11)
Dixie Grammar School

SCALES

When I have to practise scales,
My piano teacher has to say,
'You must make sure to cut your nails,
As they grow too long each day.'

I start off with C major,
An easy one that is,
Then I get into some danger,
Because I finish in a tizz.

C sharp's the next one I play,
Enharmonic of D flat,
Even though I practise all day,
I think it's upsetting the cat.

So I do it again and again,
Until I've got it right,
I'm sick of playing this game,
Oh no,
Is that a hint?
They've turned out the light.

Emily Newborough (11)
Dixie Grammar School

THE LION

His big powerful paws plod
Along the ground.
His long thin tail swishes
As he walks
His big head with his furry mane
Moves from side to side.
He roars!
His long, sharp, white teeth show.
He looked so sweet with his
Large, deep, dark eyes.
His cute, black nose.
His short, pricked ears.

Why don't people like them?
Ahh!

Sophie Comley (11)
Dixie Grammar School

THE DEPARTURE LOUNGE

Roll out the dull brown carpet,
Sprinkle in some soft grey seats.
Add some litter and a buggy (or two).
Stir in some women's dainty handbags
Beat in some big, heavy rucksacks.
Whisk in the bookshop, sweet shop, the lot.
Slowly mix the 'quiet' readers.
Knead in the sleeping babies,
Season with big, screaming kids.
Then blend in the small children.
Pour in the bus loads of people.
Bake whilst watching the planes fly away.
Leave until you hear the 'Bing-bong',
Serve with an up, up and away.

Georgina Swain (12)
Dixie Grammar School

DREAMING

'Hold me! Hug me! Love me!' The pattern is repeated.
'Care for me!' She cries, not in her voice, but in her eyes.
Her face, a flying bird, reaching for the clouds in a dream.
He hopes plummet as her dream is softly broken.
'Leave me here, I only want to play' whispers her smile.
Time is eternity, she's reminded, play is eternity.
Turning and tossing, she's tormented with failure.
'Leave me alone' she cries, she fights for peace, in a life.
The life that never spoke, but emotions are endless.
She's woken by her mother, who says, 'Dear, you were only dreaming.'

Jonathan Fowler (12)
Dixie Grammar School

ALICE'S WONDERLAND

In this faraway land,
Things are not as they seem.
When you think they're blue,
They make themselves green.

Do you know of this place?
It is called Wonderland.
I know it quite well.
It's really quite grand.

There's a Cheshire cat,
He gets into trouble.
He smiles a lot.
You can see double.

There's a Jabberwocky,
He's really nice too.
He looks really strange,
His wings are bright blue.

It's a wonderful place.
You should go there sometime.
That's why I made up
This lovely rhyme.

Susan Tweed (11)
Dixie Grammar School

LOOKING BACK

Young, hopeful, prospect of success,
With a dodgy haircut,
He looks tired and grey, in the middle of London,
Ignoring his fans, looking back at the stadium.

Anthony Lazarus (12)
Dixie Grammar School

LAST WEEKEND

Oops, I've done something wrong!
What will my mum say?
Will she scream and shout?
Probably.
What am I gonna do?
I didn't do it.
Yes I did.
Oh why did I do it?
It's my fault, I know,
Time, please take me back
I beg you.
Give me one more chance to put things right,
'Cause if I can't, guilt will hunt me down,
On purpose?
You bet.
Fear will restrain me from confessing to what I know I did.

Oh why did I do it?
It's my fault I know,
Time please take me back,
I beg you.

Danielle Burgham (13)
Dixie Grammar School

CONFUSING

The wolf looks confused
he is staring at the man.
Who is in the background looking
at the wolf, looking confused.
Maybe they are confusing each other.

Peter O'Brien (12)
Dixie Grammar School

MY MAD FAMILY

I have a kangaroo, a bouncy kangaroo.
A sweet, soft, kind and generous carer.
I call her my mum.

I have a moose, a fast, furious moose.
Weird and thick.
I call him my dad.

I have a dog, a soft, cuddly dog.
She is very kind to the household.
And has a thing for grapes.
She's humorous.
I call her my sister.

I have a baby monkey,
He is very naughty, he has a pink face,
With blue eyes.
I call him my mischievous brother.

I have a giraffe, a tall giraffe,
She is funny and fury with her multicoloured coat.
I call her Cathy.

Anna Plester (11)
Dixie Grammar School

A MATTER OF MINUTES

Hustle, bustle, the town is alive
With people enjoying life.
But all it takes
Is a matter of minutes
Then death reigns over the silence
Of the smouldering remains.

Luke Franklin (12)
Dixie Grammar School

GREY-BLUE

Dolphin.
Amongst the grey-blue sea
Its grey-blue nose, pointing,
Pointing, to the grey-blue sky.
Going to rain grey-blue droplets of water.
Suddenly, a grey-blue flash,
It speeds along, moving away,
Away from the grey-blue mass,
That is hunting it.
Scared for its life.
The grey-blue flash is spent;
Grey-blue turns to crimson . . .

Tristan Davies (12)
Dixie Grammar School

FAME

Four bubbly girls
smiling, laughing, having fun,
with their friends.
Their faces have
a smile from ear to ear,
so happy with the attention they are getting,
posing, ready for the flash of the cameras
Fame at last.

Anna Brosnan (12)
Dixie Grammar School

A Night Out On The Town

Having fun with his friends and his girlfriend, Amy,
Laughing and joking,
but is he really happy?
Being famous is not easy even at night.
Even clubs in London have fans.
What is Amy thinking?
Is she happy or is she jealous?
He is so good looking,
With so many fans.
Will he be loyal?
Who knows?

Anne Mackey (12)
Dixie Grammar School

The Fairground

Roll out a green field.
Add a mixture of rides.
Stir in lots of people.
Sprinkle rubbish everywhere.
Mix in burger bars and candyfloss stalls.
Boil up the excitement.
Grate bright lights over the rides.
Beat in the shouting.
Knead together well.
Serve with lost voices.

Lorna Jones (12)
Dixie Grammar School

WALES

Setting off at ten in the morning,
Should arrive at one.

Off to see Nannie and Grampy
In the August sun.

Only just out of Hinckley
Several of those cars have come.

Past us in the green car,
Rides a friend of my mum's.

Out on the motorway,
Nannie, here we come!

Go to sleep for the next two hours,
Just over the Welsh border.

Monmouth tunnels.
Brynglas tunnels.

Cardiff.
Barry . . . here!

Hello Nannie.
Hello Grampy.

Back again.
Yippee!

Sophie Hooper (12)
Dixie Grammar School

FOOTBALL

Football is your game
You give the game your all.
Your only love in life,
Is 11 men and a ball.

Football is your game,
Rugby is not as good.
Everyone says, 'You're a pain'
When you walk in covered in mud.

Football is your game,
Sometimes you play in the rain.
Your friends say, 'You're not sane,'
But you're determined to make fame.

Football is your game,
And when you are playing for United,
And the cash is rolling in,
Remember you don't always have to win.

Oliver Moore (12)
Dixie Grammar School

SEASIDE

Roll down a golden beach,
Arrange screaming children making sandcastles on top.
Add the sun and a pint of water,
Not forgetting a gallon of salt.
Chill an ice-cream van
Beat in screeching seagulls,
Place a boat on the horizon,
Then chill out in the cool sea.

John Matthews (13)
Dixie Grammar School

STAFFROOM

Roll out a cosy staffroom,
Mix in some chatting teachers,
Add some boiled yo-yos,
Whisk in some maths books.
Take out of the school, and place on a floured playground,
Knead in some detention slips,
Make a hole in the middle and crack in a steaming headmaster,
Leave to prove
Bake in a hot school,
Serve with pickled children.

Andrew James Dowsett (12)
Dixie Grammar School

THE CIRCUS

Take one large tent,
Add a roaring lion with a nervous tamer.
Stir in with some flexible acrobats.
Mix in a circus master.
Blend in rings of fire.
Knead in the elephants until it's complete.
Finally, cook up an audience, then
Mash up the fun.
Sprinkle in some excitement and what have you got:
A taste of the circus.

Natalie Gillett (13)
Dixie Grammar School

SISTERS

Sisters, sisters are a pain.
They really, really are.
Wherever you're going,
However you're feeling.
They'll nag you in the car.

Playing in a football match,
Just scored a wonderful goal.
Sister, sister,
Will be on the pitch,
Telling you what's to be told.

Halfway through the Latin test,
Whatever you've told her,
How much.
Sister, sister will be in the room,
Telling you the answers or such.

If you're trying to do your homework,
Struggling on your maths.
Sister, sister,
Will come charging in,
Testing you your times tables and such.

Sisters, sisters,
Look up to you,
My brother, hero and such.
It really can't be that bad at all,
Because they've got taste.
Of course!

Mark Harrison (11)
Dixie Grammar School

My Friends

I had a friend called Anne
She hit herself with a pan.
She had to see the doctor
But in a cupboard he locked her.
She stayed in there for days
It gave her time to sort out her ways.
But when she came out
She started to shout.
So that was the end of her.

I had a friend called Pat
She really liked to chat.
She talked to me in lessons
And after school sessions.
She talks to me on the phone
She talks to me about musical tones.
She talks to me about a competition she won
She said it was really quite fun.
But after that,
She never stopped to chat.

Chloe Lees (11)
Dixie Grammar School

The Thing

It was one day in class,
When someone brought something in.
It was big and made of brass.
And polished and shone like a pin.

We didn't know it was threatening,
Until someone turned it on.
Then it was something we were dreading.
We all wished it was gone.

This thing was made with terror,
It was also scanning the area.
It was looking for innocent souls.
Which through them it could make a hole.

Then someone had the courage to turn it off,
His name was Jack he was rather a boff.
Now Jack is rather a hero,
No more is he a zero.

William Davies (11)
Dixie Grammar School

MIGRATION

Away the birds fly,
High into the sky.
Escaping the winter bleak,
A warmer climate to seek.

Over the mountains steep,
No time for any sleep.
Over the everlasting ocean,
They glide with their winged motion.

Over the sandy desert plain,
Away the pools of water drain.
Away from the frozen north,
Their wings beating back and forth.

After thousands of miles they land,
Coming to rest on baking sand.
They have a few short months and weeks,
To have their young and fill their beaks.

Thomas Smith (11)
Dixie Grammar School

SCHOOL DAY

English is first,
It's a strange little thing.
All those adjectives and verbs
And spelling those complicated words.

It's music now,
We'll be singing or playing,
A keyboard or flute.
Making wonderful sounds like pip, pip, toot, toot.

Before lunch it's maths.
Adding, subtracting algebra, fractions
And multiplication.
Come on have some consideration.

The last two periods of the day.
We have art and do some painting.
Today I made a colour wheel
And did some paintings that looked like you could feel them.

It's time to go home,
Hip, hip hooray and when I get home,
There's no homework for me,
For tomorrow is Saturday, you see.

Aimée Lockley (11)
Dixie Grammar School

ANIMAL OLYMPICS

Owl observed the Olympics,
Tiger tiptoed to the trampoline,
Baboon bounced near to the banner,
Snake slithered across the sand pit,
Antelope ambled onto the apparatus,
Giraffe jumped as he threw the javelin,
Rabbit ran the race,
Hare hopped over the hurdles,
Lion leapt over the line,
Parrot presented the prizes.

Rachael Corbett (12)
Dixie Grammar School

THE SEASIDE

Sprinkle out some golden sand,
Pour in three pints of water,
And shake in some salt.
Beat in the seagulls.
And mix in some relaxing families,
Having a picnic on the sand.
Add some buildings to the mix,
Put in a burger bar oozing with people,
The amusement arcade with lots of flashing lights,
And the ice-cream stall.

Alex Deamon (13)
Dixie Grammar School

SPIDER IN THE SHOWER

I'm in the shower singing away,
There's no need to rush, its Saturday.
I reach for the soap and what do I see?
An eight-legged creature looking at me.

'Help! Help!' I scream 'Please get it out!'
The spider starts to run about,
It's ugly and brown and runs quite fast,
It nearly goes down the plughole at last.

All of a sudden it climbs back out,
I start once again to scream and shout,
I was scared and shocked and in a state,
And really starting to dread my fate.

When, here comes my hero to save the day,
She's brave and washes the spider away,
I'm so relieved it's gone away,
She was the hero that saved the day.

Katy Mensforth (11)
Dixie Grammar School

MY ANIMAL FAMILY

I have a bear, a big furry bear,
He virtually controls the family.
He loves meat and moans if he is annoyed.
He works most of the day.
I call him Dad.

I also have a dolphin.
Like my bear, she works most of the day too
She is intelligent and learns quickly.
She is gentle.
I call her Mum.

I have a black sheep, one that's quite opposite of me.
She does not like logical games.
She learns slowly and likes annoying me.
But she goes as mad as a hatter if I annoy her.
I call her sister.

Then there's me,
I know what I am.
I am the owl.

Kingman Cheng (11)
Dixie Grammar School

MY MUSICAL HOUSEHOLD

My brother plays rave music all day,
It's loud, it's strong, like he wants to be.
But with the sound turned down,
He really is thoughtful and calm.

My mother listens to classical music,
She listens while she is working.
She can move with speed or,
Be slow or calm in a crisis.

My father listens to music from the seventies,
They bring back memories.
As he travels along the motorways,
He has his music for company.

My favourite music is the piano,
I play a piece of music to suit my mood.
When I play a joyful piece, I am happy,
When I play a slow, sad piece, I am sad.

Maxine Smith (11)
Dixie Grammar School

THE WATCHER

I am the inspector, watching the cars made,
watching robots who do not need to be paid.
They took over from people, working,
while the robots, who are new, are working,
I watch and gaze,
like it is a daze,
waiting for something to happen in here,
like a fire, or explosion, changing from being here, to not.

Alex Hall (12)
Dixie Grammar School

HUGO

Innocent and sweet it may appear,
it owns a cute and loving face.
Look deep into its wondering eyes,
he longs for a walk,
in a field with a ball and a lead.
A hug does not have to go amiss,
so stroke his tactile, warm and silky coat.

Katie Barnett (12)
Dixie Grammar School

ESCAPE

As he ran, stumbling through the trees, he heard a shout,
Then a shot, and he dived into the undergrowth,
Pain shot up his leg and he cried out in pain,
He crouched down low, avoiding their watchful eyes.

As the hunters stalk nearer, he pulls himself through the bushes,
He hears the hunters talking and then nothing
Except the click of a gun loading.
The gun rings out, the bullet cracks into the tree above him.

He scrambled up the slope and falls into a hollow,
As he lay on the ground and watched the hunters unseen
He cocked his gun,
And fired.

David Lloyd (14)
Hind Leys Community College

FORGETTING TIME

Sitting down whilst it's so quiet around,
Not bothering to look at my watch,
as time doesn't seem to matter,
If I listen there is noise but not noise which is noisy.
Birds chattering, the silver water trickling beside me,
Autumn leaves blowing in the breeze,
little grey and red squirrels running from the trees,
I suddenly remember what I have to do that day,
I get up to walk away back to the humming noise of the busy town.

Hayley Bancroft (15)
Hind Leys Community College

BESS!

You used to run through the fields like a bullet out of a gun.
You used to chase the rabbits, you sure had them on the run.
But now I'm older and so are you and when you're time's up
I'll be thinking of you.
But let's just think about the good times we used to have when
you were a pup.
I used to push you round in my pushchair, that's right we were a
right pair,
I used to try beating you at running but only now I know you are
very cunning.
And when you and Jud had the pups I cried with joy, but boy they
weren't as nice as you pair.
It's Wednesday 9th October I've just found out Bess, you've died
And I hope you think of me in every stride,
I'm lying on the carpet looking in the air, tell me Bess are you there?
I know you're still there inside but it's not the same when you're
not by my side.
So now here's my prayer from me to you
God bless you Bess and God will be there with you.

Jodie Hill (14)
Hind Leys Community College

HALLOWE'EN

Blood-curdling screams tear through the night
While witches and wolves look on in delight,
For all are gathered here on this Hallow's eve night.

So many people, the town not forsaken
After the tribe of the dead awaken.
So many deaths, such a terrible price,
For all who are to be a sacrifice.

The innocent hide, lock themselves away,
While vampires wait and watch for their prey,
Drawing ever closer, day by day,
Waiting until you look the other way,
Waiting, ever waiting, until they . . .

Attack!

Laura Roberts (14)
Hind Leys Community College

WATER

Clouds bursting,
Rain pouring.
Water dripping,
Puddles splashing.

Taps running,
Baths overflowing.
Steaming windows,
Water freezing.

Rivers flowing,
Waves crashing.
Brooks trickling,
Waterfalls falling.

Icebergs floating,
Ships sailing.
Fountains spraying,
Pools filling.

Laura Evans (14)
Hind Leys Community College

AUTUMN

The splendid leaves of autumn,
Of gold, maroon and brown have all blown from the trees,
And to our dismay and disbelief, lie trampled and discoloured,
Upon the wet and muddy ground.

Can we remember how beautiful they were,
The sun filtering through the leaves,
Casting shadows here and there,
Sometimes keeping the sun's bright rays from penetrating everywhere.

The leaves have gone now, winter is on it's way,
And we must wait until the spring,
And then once more we will see the buds,
The trees will blossom once again to bring us pleasure as before.

Thomas Halcarz (14)
Hind Leys Community College

YOUNG LOVE

Love is just a blind eye
I see what others don't.
I think of you all the time
I feel my eyes fill with tears
Because I have fallen in love with you
And now I never want to part my love from you.

Martina O'Donnell (14)
Hind Leys Community College

FIRE

Fire lit up the night,
Like an angry dragon
Puffing billows of smoke
Over the sleeping town.
Slowly it creeps through the darkness
Deliberate, destructive, determined.
Engulfing the sky.
Ash flies like showers of golden rain.
Through the roaring flames
A blackened twisted wreck
Of burnt wood piled high.
Glows on the faces of the onlookers
The raging fire of the night.

Claire Harris (14)
Hind Leys Community College

SUNSET BEACH

The sun in the sky as hot as fire,
Beating down on your body.
The sand so white and pure
Alongside the sparkling sea.

The waves going up and down,
Boats in the distance,
I am far away in my imagination.

Lyndsey Bronwin-Shore (15)
Hind Leys Community College

BONFIRE NIGHT

Bonfire Night is so bright,
Fireworks and moon making light.

Dark blue, red and yellow flames roaring high.
Startled the youngsters standing by.

Jumping Jacks bouncing around,
Burnt-out rockets hitting the ground.

Catherine wheels spinning here and there,
Roman candles with a coloured flare.

The fire burning high and bright,
The crowd mumbles 'Oh what a sight.'

Ashley Pycroft (14)
Hind Leys Community College

WHY DOES IT NEED A TITLE?

What is the saviour of mankind?
What gets you through a long phone call?
What do you do when there's nothing else to do?
Doodle!
Everybody doodles,
It's just a way of life
If there's a pen in your hand and a note pad nearby
You just can't help it,
Can you?

Peter Walker (15)
Hind Leys Community College

THE RACE

The day had come,
The day of the race,
The pool reflected the morning sun,
Streaming through the windows.
This was what I'd been training for,
Preparing for,
Worried about.
Now it was all nerves,
The atmosphere was tense.
Only one race before I was to swim.
My hat and goggles in position,
(Fiddled with enough),
The whistle blew,
To mount the blocks,
Nerves, determination now.
I was to win,
I told myself,
As I was diving in.
Sprint all the way,
I told myself,
As not long I had to swim.
My opposition seemed ahead,
That just wouldn't do.
My arms worked faster,
My legs kicked harder,
And down the lane I flew.
I'd finished first,
I,
The best.

Claire Lockwood (14)
Hind Leys Community College

LOVE'S TOUGH

The tortures of love run through my mind.
Love's pleasures, I just cannot find.
The pain, the tears, the lonely heart.
The fear I felt when we're apart.
I can't describe the way I feel about my love for you.
You've seen me cry, you've seen me laugh, you've even
broken my heart.
But I can't explain the pain I feel deep inside my heart, it's
like a poison dart.
If only I had one more chance to prove our love's for real.
I really hope the way I feel is the way that you feel too.
We had good times and even bad but never have they been sad,
All because each one of them I spent my time with you.

Keeley Watson (14)
Hind Leys Community College

MOVING ON

It's time to go, it's time to move on.
You may not want to,
but the force is too strong.
You may cry, you may scream,
But things are not as bad as they seem.
You may smile, you may laugh,
You may go absolutely mad.
It's time to go, it's time to move on.

Kelly Sherwood (14)
Hind Leys Community College

THE WOLF DOG

You can see it walking around,
Thumping hard on the ground,
People wondering,
People staring,
People frightened,
As they hear the howling of the wolf dog.

You can hear it down in the valley,
The groaning,
The howling,
The weeping of the lonely wolf dog.

They all get scared,
You should see them,
But what about the lonely wolf dog?
He might be scared,
But then again he might be happy,
Maybe he wants friends,
Or maybe he wants nice meaty food,
But he might be a vegetarian,
Nobody knows,
Nobody cares,
Just as long as they're safe,
But what about the lonely, howling, weeping wolf dog?

Tuppence Measham
Hind Leys Community College

LOVE

Falling in love is the best thing in the world,
Holding hands, kissing and making love.

We act like birds in the springtime,
And act like rabbits in the summer,
And we cuddle up like polar bears in the winter,
But in autumn we're like leaves on the ground.

My heartbeat goes as fast as a horse running.

We were joined together like Siamese twins,
But unfortunately we were cut down the middle,
We parted,
The nights are long, the songs are quiet,
The colours are dull.

And the 12 months are now all winter.

Lisa Finney (15)
Hind Leys Community College

SNOW

Snowflakes falling all around us
floating down towards the ground.
Landing gently on the blanket of snow
looking outside at the new cold world.

It was silent except for the laughter
of the children playing outside.
On the white snow blanket
building snowmen and women with hats and scarves.

And suddenly the sun broke through
and shone down on the white snow
beginning to melt it,
like a piece of ice too warm.

The sky was clouded over
and it was time for bed.
I took one more look out of the window,
It was a winter wonderland.

Tracey Whitworth (14)
Hind Leys Community College

I HATE THE DARK

I hate the dark
I can't close my eyes at night.
I turn on my light
And get a big fright
There's my mask on my wall.
I turned off my light
And got back into bed.
I looked towards the window
The moon was shining through
It was making the room silvery.
Wait!
Is there someone out there?
I walked to the window
My legs shaking
My hands sweating
I opened the curtains
It was only a tree.

Lynsey Gamble (14)
Hind Leys Community College

ROSES

To walk forever
in a field of roses.
The skylark's song,
singing in my ears.
The wind blows through my hair
like a person's hands,
Carrying the spirits of friends, family, and
others unknown to my existence.
One day I'll be the wind
and blow through someone's hair.
In a field of roses,
where you could walk forever.

Amy Bartram (14)
Hind Leys Community College

SNOW

Fluttering down to earth from heaven.
Twinkling in the morning sun.
Delicate and soft
Melting in the warm fingers of a child.
Cold, but with that warm atmosphere.
I love the snow, smooth like silk.
Soft, like a big, cuddly teddy bear
Oh snow! Oh snow!

Please snow!

Amy Melbourne (15)
Hind Leys Community College

CHILD-LIKE

When you are a child,
You are treated like a child.
When you are a teenager,
You are patronised like a child.
When you are an adult,
You are treated like a child
by your own parents.
When you are elderly,
You are treated like a child
in your nursing home.
So maybe we will all stay young,
even when we are old.

Leanne Walker (14)
Hind Leys Community College

AIRA FORCE

Eyes gaze upon it as it falls,
the roaring sound echoes in your ears.
We listen and we watch,
as these magnificent falls defuse into one another,
crashing and spewing against the high risen rocks.
Perhaps it's telling us something
but without any words,
just thoughts.
The sun is high but you feel refreshed
as the spray gently cools your face.

Angela Gubb (14)
Hind Leys Community College

NIGHT

Black, silver,
Stars twinkling, shining.
Each star waiting to tell a different person's story of life,
happiness, joy.
Difference each one unique.
Floating in mid-darkness
Sparkle like millions of big bright eyes,
guiding you through the night.
One moon
A single smile and you know,
Someone up there is watching your journey home;
Safely.

Carla Wilford (15)
Hind Leys Community College

IT

I walked in the room
It was cold and dark
I felt I was being watched.
I walked into the back room
And closed the window, got my torch out my bag
The batteries were flat.
I sat on a chair, nervous
I heard a bang upstairs
I ran for the door
It was locked
I looked round frantic,
I saw two eyes peering at me from across the hall
It ran at me.

Adam Sleigh (14)
Hind Leys Community College

HALLOWE'EN

Welcome to the spirit of Hallowe'en night
The supernatural's time to fright
Luminous pumpkins burning bright
Casting shadows in the night.

Figures enter through the wall
Flying, whizzing down the hall
Disappearing up the stairs
Were they really ever there?

Witches flying in the darkness
Near a pale, full moon
Spooks lurking in the dimness
It will all be over soon.

Sometimes I really wonder
Could all this be true?
But this eeriness surrounds you
It may soon be haunting you!

Kerry Sibson (14)
Hind Leys Community College

QUIVER

Your eyes see straight through me
Your stare makes me quake.
Your mouth makes me tremble,
Your teeth make me shake,
You are my angel, my love, my light,
You are my morn, my noon, my night.
You are my star that shines so bright.

Matthew Baker (14)
Hind Leys Community College

CHANGING WEATHER

The weather's changing
The summer's gone,
The leaves are falling one by one.

The lakes are freezing,
The birds are flying home,
Walking past the fields on my own.

The surrounding's changing,
The grass turns brown
Animals in hibernation,
Now none left in the town.

The nights grow shorter
As the dark sets in,
Now it's here, the winter will begin.

Kerry Smith (14)
Hind Leys Community College

MAYBE

Maybe I could be a bird
Fly high in the blue blanket
No rules, no worries,
Sleep where you like
Then move on
Soaring through the people's world
A dreamy lifestyle
Freedom.

Sara Monk (15)
Hind Leys Community College

MOTORWAY

Three lanes of madness
Sometimes even four
Watch the miles fly by
Put your foot to the floor.

Lining up on the grid
On junction twenty-four
Looking for a space to go
Put your foot to the floor

Racing along the motorway
Everyone wanting more
Ford, Audi, Mercedes
Put your foot to the floor

The needle moves up
To ninety or more
When will it stop?
Put your foot to the floor

Red lights ahead
As cars start to brake
Too late to avoid
Dead!

Benjamin Nudd (14)
Hind Leys Community College

RUGBY

As the kicker kicks the ball,
My team and I one and all.
Charge down the field to attack,
The enemy team and push them back,

I tackle one, I tackle two,
I tackle everyone who's wearing blue,
We win the ball, we all advance,
And then we have a brilliant chance,

A line-out throw for me to catch,
I jump, I move my hands and snatch,
The rugby ball its oval figure
And then I run with rage and vigour.

The tri line's there it's in my sight,
And then I run towards the right.
And as I dive I hear the sound,
Hooray! The rugby ball is on the ground.

Daniel Rourke (15)
Hind Leys Community College

BLOWING OFF THE LEAVES

The wind rushed through the trees
Blowing off the leaves,
Driving into the bushes
And blowing off the leaves.

The weather took a turn for the worst
And blew off all the leaves,
The storm came down and wrecked the tree
And off blew all the leaves.

The tree was strong in summer so the wind struggled
And couldn't blow off the leaves,
But in the autumn it was a different matter
As the trees are ripped to a tatter.

Simon Adcock (14)
Hind Leys Community College

WINGS

The giant metal tube,
No wings, just an engine.
The huge thing,
Only a tiny computer chip to make it move,
No pilot, nothing, no flight crew at all.

Soon to go, just closing the door.
Wheels retracting, hovering above the floor.
Turning into place, heading for the runway.
It hasn't failed yet,
Must be the fact that we had to clean it.

A shiver running down my spine;
It jets across above the ground.
Lifts its nose and rises into the morning sky.
500 people on the flying tank.

It soars above just like a bird.
Gliding so silently.
Climbing in the sky. Then it speeds up and disappears.
It doesn't look safe to me.
I'm glad I use my wings.

Alexander Shaw (14)
Hind Leys Community College

IS SHE, ISN'T SHE?

Is she, isn't she when will we know,
When will the bump begin to show?
Morning sickness, feeling tired,
Blood tests, hospital visits,
A new person begins to grow,
A scan reveals, baby playing with toes!

Boy or girl, nobody knows?
Trousers too tight
A bump now in sight!
Uncomfortable feelings, was that a kick?
No more feeling sick!
Visits to midwife, hospital too,
Fingers swelling, ankles too,
Time to rest.

Knitting needles click,
Cots, pushchairs, lots to pick,
Baby clothes, nappies,
Everything's so small!
Terry's or disposables when will it crawl?

Time's nearly up,
D-Day nearing!
What shall we call it? Names keep appearing,

Dad's getting nervous,
Mum is too, who will baby look like,
Uncle John or Auntie Sue?

Sarah Besant (15)
Hind Leys Community College

ADRENALIN RUSH

The cogs are whirring faster now,
brain cells killing insignificant debris
as I rack my brains for thought.
Why I ask repetitively,
put myself through this tortuous ride,
as I crumpled the ticket I bought.

My stomach is doing somersaults,
as the hissing ride pushes off,
oil-infested fumes waft my way.
The rapid increase in speed sends my adrenalin rocket high,
the ride suspended at a stupendous height,
to my dismay.

Formidably we dropped, the cold bit at my cheeks,
my eyes snapped shut,
as my clench encrusted the bar.

The G-force was incredible, tears streaked my temples,
my stomach trembled crazily in a pit of terrified mush.
My flesh was lodged inconveniently against the vibrating machine
of death,
my ribs felt fit to crush.

Heat flared through my veins,
as the mechanical structure jerked to a halt,
relief was written on my face.
My legs failed me,
I gripped the cart for balance,
my heart was saying again,
My stomach leave this place.

Amy Butler (14)
Hind Leys Community College

FRIENDS

Friends, friends are so cool,
they always come around when you are down,
and cheer you up until you're as happy as a clown.

Friends help you with your work as well as making
you talk!
With your mates you have a laugh because one has
a neck like a giraffe.

After school you can hang around and make them do things,
they really hate.

Rich or poor you can still
love 'em all!

Sophia Thorpe (14)
Hind Leys Community College

BOY IN A BOX

(This poem is based on a newspaper article
about a boy who was treated in this way)

Bound and gagged
Confined in a cardboard box,
Bent double in total darkness
For days and days on end.

Like a little alien
With misshapen head
Lumps, a black eye
A gaping gash in his skull.

Tortured, cigarette-scarred body
In a cardboard prison
Unable to break free
Praying to be saved.

Finally his prayers are answered
Freed by a passing neighbour.
Despite life-threatening injuries
He survived the trauma.

Linda Bevan (14)
Hind Leys Community College

ENGLISH HOMEWORK

I have to write a poem
but I don't know what to say
I've got to try and make it rhyme
in any sort of way

Try to use some verbs
try to use some nouns
I don't really care
how this poem sounds.

What a waste of time
trying to make words rhyme
I just want to have some fun
is that such a crime?

So now I sit and try to think
of something good to write
I have to write a poem
before I say goodnight.

Rachel Varney (14)
Hind Leys Community College

WITCHES' BREW

If I tell you this recipe,
Please do not be sick on me.
But this is the witches' best brew.
The first thing you need is some squashed slugs and suede and
last night's old vindaloo.
Mix altogether and season with pepper and add some more of
these things.
Carrots, mud, coal and a dirty old mole will give it some texture
but you also need some lovely flavour, so why don't you add
some tomato, potato and an arm of a waiter.
As you know Hallowe'en is soon,
Get making this brew and you might end up howling at the moon.

Rebecca Cluer (15)
Hind Leys Community College

FRIENDS THEY'RE JUST LIKE THAT

Friends, how more loyal can they get?
I mean, they're always there for you
So supportive and talkative
You can tell them almost anything
From your deepest, darkest secrets to the things that just pop
Into your head and scream
Oh fun, so much fun, those rushes of energy and bursts of laughter
Will they ever go . . . *no!*
Through thick and thin and all that stuff
They're always there
Because friends, they're just like that.

Kate Faucheux (14)
Hind Leys Community College

GT-24

Viper, Merc, McLaren and Porsche,
Lined up on the grid,
Drivers ready for the race,
A race of sheer force.

Off they go! Away, away!
Pace and power, precision,
Viper pulls into the lead,
A race that lasts a day.

McLaren pulls into the pit,
The team are there with speed,
Off with the tyres, on with the lights,
The new driver's in for his fit.

The Porsche pulls out, the engine's failed,
The driver jumps out and swears,
They try to get it going again,
A whirr, it putts, the engineer wailed.

The Viper drives up to the line,
The chequered flag's in sight,
The driver's on the podium,
'This champagne's all mine!'

James Newton (14)
Hind Leys Community College

WAR ON A SUMMER AFTERNOON

The green soldiers, standing tall and proud,
Each wearing a silver jewelled crown of dew
Then cut off in their prime,
As the groundsman forces them to a uniform length,

Then as the sun climbs to its peak,
The white men walk out, to fight their duel
A duel of willow and leather
The tide of the battle swinging, like the scarlet ball.

And then they stop,
The white men forgetting their duel and leaving the battleground
And the green lieutenants.
To annihilate the cheese, egg and spam sandwiches
The regiment of 22 then advance
Attacking the cream cakes and doughnuts
With the most venom seen all day.

Then the Titans return to their war,
The heat of the battle grows
And the optimum and the ultimate shots are fired,
The beamer hits the throat
The crunch of broken toes from the yorker
The tumbling and clattering of leather into stumps
At last under the setting sun
The petrified rabbit enters the stage
The crimson sphere hits the deck
And then the heart-stopping sound as it hits the stumps
The warriors walk off as a golden duck graces the scoreboard.

Matthew Foster (15)
Hind Leys Community College

COLOURS

The sun, the moon,
a big round balloon.
A banana, a melon,
a flower, a lemon.
A car, a van,
the breadcrumbs on ham.
This word rhymes with mellow,
it's the colour yellow.

The horrors, the pains,
the aeroplanes.
The bombs, the guns,
the screaming mums.
The injured, the dead,
this colour is red.

The beginning, now the end,
And not one friend, they've gone,
disappeared!
Just what I feared.
Some just went,
while others die.
And on its own,
stood the weeping eye.

The light, the dark,
no kids in the park.
The living, the dead,
that's all to be said.
It rhymes with sack,
it's the colour black.

Danielle Grady (14)
Hind Leys Community College

WALLACE

Wallace, a weary, young male cat, awakens from a deep sleep.
As he stretches and looks around, he spots it.
The white ball, there in the middle of the floor, lies still.
Mid-yawn he stops to jump off the work surface.
He creeps up and watches his prey.
Then he pounces.
With one leap he's on top of the ball and scooting around the
living room.

After a small time, of a young cat's life,
Wallace becomes tired of the ball.
He has his dinner then decides he wants to go out.
Wallace sits by the front door waiting and yelling for someone
to let him out.

At last, it happens. he's free.
He saunters out into the cold night air and looks around.
She's there, by the tree, waiting.
Filled with excitement he walks over to her.
Wallace and Domino have known each other since he was a
kitten and enjoys his nights with her.

Dawn comes and the cats part.
They go their separate ways until the next night, when they shall
meet again.
A night on the prowl leaves a young cat tired and hungry.

Charlotte Montague (14)
Hind Leys Community College

THE FAIR

The fair was so much fun,
But now the fair is gone.
The rides were really cool,
And we always look like fools.
Always on the Mexican eggs,
We get really dizzy heads.
Seems too empty without it there,
The always funny Dono fair.

Amy Wilson (14)
Hind Leys Community College

TEARDROPS

Within each tear is a memory,
which haunts us while we sleep.
They'll stay with us forever,
like the friends we couldn't keep.

Within each tear is a fear,
which slowly tears us apart.
They'll stay with us forever,
living to break the heart.

Within each tear is a thought,
which makes us wonder why.
They'll stay with us forever,
until the day we die.

Sally Lee (17)
Longslade Community College

ALONE

Alone, sitting in the corner of the room,
His eyes pale with the dullness of the light,
The skin forming heavily around his hands that shake constantly.
Unsteady,
His face soft, changing with age, as the years pass,
Alone, not a person to talk to,
Only the square senseless screen of the empty TV,
As it plays to no one, only Grandad,
I arrive, so happy to see his face,
His eyes change, pleasure surrounds him,
We talk,
His face glows with the happiness inside him,
He laughs, a soft amusing laugh,
The heat rushes to his face,
The jokes he makes, the stories told of years passed,
I see him sitting there, 84 in age, making jokes,
I laugh,
But then I wonder, the people he's lost, his wife, his brother, his friends
The trauma of the war he faced, when I was non-existent,
I just can't imagine how he coped,
And now he sits, laughing, but knowing that when I leave him,
                                        he will be alone again,
One day, although I hate to think it,
Maybe he will be with the ones he's lost,
I would miss him, as he's unique, a glorious person,
But now as I go, reluctant to do so,
He sits, watching time pass,
The clock ticking,
Years going by,
Memories present,
Alone.

Rebecca Platts (14)
Longslade Community College

A Smile

A smile costs nothing, but gives much
It enriches those who receive
Without making poorer those who give
It takes but a moment
But the memory of it sometimes lasts forever
None is so rich or mighty
That he can get along without it
And none is so poor
But that he can be made rich by it
A smile creates happiness in the home
Fosters goodwill in business
And is the countersign of friendship
It brings rest to the weary
Cheer to the discouraged
Sunshine to the sad
And it is nature's best antidote for trouble
Yet it cannot be bought, begged, borrowed or stolen
For it is something that is of no value
To anyone until it is given away
Some people are too tired to give you a smile
Give them one of yours
As none needs a smile so much
As he who has no more to give.

Zoe Plant (15)
Longslade Community College

THE SEA

Unpredictable, independent,
Like life itself:
Peaceful, yet moody,
Relaxing, yet forceful.
Uncontrolled. Powerful.

With passion it rushes
Back and forth,
Back and forth.
As if wanting to explore new lands
But apprehensive of what may lay ahead.
Back and forth,
Back and forth.

The blue unknown,
Like the eyes of a stranger.
With a calming beauty.

Its continuous rhythm,
Like an ongoing heartbeat.
Never ending; an eternal life.

Its sparkle,
A reflection of its spirit,
Like thousands of pure sapphires,
Hanging on an evening sky.

Through storms, through calm.
Never ending. Determined to carry on.
Like a make believe hero, battling on.
Year after year, generation after generation.

Unhindered, unchanged.
Free like a bird,
Swirling, turning
With a grace of its own.

Emma Hutchins (15)
Longslade Community College

OCTOBER 31ST

Hellish echoes and cryptic motion fly
Over the boiling, churning seas
Bringing power from a force so great
It would force God to His knees.

These are the gales that kiss the mist
With the dismal call of the crow
Sending distress and demise across the bleak moors
To the hell-holes deep down below.

Below the earth the caverns lie
Filled with greed and hate
Evil spectres forming covens
Outside Hell's rusted gate.

Beware of the demons rising from beneath
With claws as black as night
Beware the horror as thick as concrete
Struggle over it with all your might.

Leaving Hell now, over the icy mountains
Ascending as high as a kite
Away from evil and its loathsome counterparts
And soaring deeper into the night.

Jamie Carr (15)
Longslade Community College

POTENTIAL

The man I know I could be.
The boy I am stuck as.
Every day starts the same,
Putting my face on. Having it eaten off.

One day I'll leave without it.
Face the world as me.
Not go back as you or you.
Not changing. Just the face.

Under it lies a devil.
Red and fuming, putrid infestations
Fill the chasm, mangled, pulsating,
Dark red throbs, throbs, pulsates,
Seeps, oozes, fills the open
Spaces.

Pete Tatham (17)
Longslade Community College

KALEIDOSCOPE OF DREAMS

In my dreams I see a shape,
A shape that's always changing,
In my dreams I see a wheel,
A wheel that's always turning.
My dreams are sharp in focus,
Yet everything's a blur,
Reality and dreams are merging,
Yet now it's all so clear.

My life's a vast mixed palette,
Of ever-changing colours,
They blend into each other,
Divide, are one again.
Bright, strong and vivid,
Mingling where they touch.
United are my life and dreams,
But oh so far apart.

Leanne Hill (14)
Loughborough High School

FOR THOUGHT

When the land has all but gone,
and pollution fills the skies.

When the hills are mountains of waste,
and the rivers run scorched and dry.

No stretch of golden sands to the eye,
but oil covered beaches and birds left to die.

No trees to protect; a smog-filled sky,
a heat intense -how can we survive?

Global disasters; too many; too often,
greed, disrupting life's sensitive balance - forgotten.

Victoria Mulcahy (14)
Loughborough High School

KALEIDOSCOPE

Deep, deep down in my kaleidoscope
Are nice bright colours gleaming back at me
Orange, purple, pink and green
Are twisting and turning round the bends of life
To something bright
Or something dull in the depth of life
The colours all merge again and again
As they travel through the different phases of life from year to year
The colours grow rapidly from a child to an adult
As they turn around and around the surface of their earth
Rattling and shaking like rice in a tin
Or rain drops falling gently on the window within
Colours and patterns change and grow
They become older and wiser straight through to the middle of their life
Where the pictures turn to greater happiness
But the colours gradually fade
And the patterns slowly slow down
Years and years pass
The colours have grown from new to old
Just waiting now till life has to come to an end
And as it does everything turns black
Black like it is when the lights are out at the very end of the day
Everything is gone and will never ever come again
The colours have represented a life
They were bright but now they are gone
Deep in the depth of darkness
A life is gone again.

Victoria Hacking (14)
Loughborough High School

KALEIDOSCOPE

A kaleidoscope reminds me
Of everything I know.
Many different colours,
That help the world to lie.

A deep blue shows me the sea,
Looking serene and graceful.
On a sleepy summer evening,
Who knows how many graves lie below?

Bright red are the berries.
In the autumn hedgerows,
Succulent and tempting for all the birds and beasts,
But such bitter poison in each mouthful.

Glistening green is the dewy morning grass,
That proves so lush for the cattle softly grazing,
And the long stalks of the insects' world
Help predators hide while their victims perish.

A burning orange is the setting of the sun.
Its fading light signals the end of the day,
Followed by the hurrying footsteps of the night.
Now devils and demons fill children's dreams.

Out of the inky blackness comes,
The violet that is dawn.
As death's cloak is lifted from our minds,
The warm yellow sunlight comes flooding in,

And a new day is born.

Katherine Woodhead (14)
Loughborough High School

THE BONFIRE

Fire, free, flying far following the night sky,
Golden as the sun, yet red as blood.
Like a monster devouring everything in its path,
There is no escape from the inevitable flames.
Harshly forcing their way past everyone and everything,
As it rides passionately on through the forest.

The children gaze at its awesome beauty,
As it swirls, soaring swiftly above the horizon.
Gleaming against the hills in the distance far away.
It hands out its consoling and comforting warmth.
Lighting the fields for its admirers who stare:
Entranced by the fantastic but dangerous creature.

Tori Dance (14)
Loughborough High School

KALEIDOSCOPE

Exploding colours,
   Like ripples from a pebble in a pond,
Hypnotising movements,
   Disappearing into the core,
A Ferris wheel whirling round and round
   Mirrored prisms of light,
Changing the coloured edges,
   Synchronised shapes and patterns,
All dancing with ribbons of colour,
   Each new pattern,
Shows an unseen kaleidoscopic beauty,

Lost in a fantasy world!

Samantha Green (12)
Loughborough High School

THE GHOST OTTER

Why do the willows rustle o'
When the sun is brightly shining so?
And why indeed does the ripple spread
When not a beast has moved its head?
How can the playful otter cry
When all of them long ago did die?

Can it be another born?
Or perhaps still a ghostly mourn
Of the happy days when river songs
Were sung of otters, grouped in throngs
And men sat quietly in their boats
To hear the otters in the moats.

'Tis a lonely otter boy,
Stuffed to make a hunting toy,
Or a trophy if you please,
Stuffed with wool and old dry peas.
Sitting in a roomy stable,
'Lot 51' on an old oak table.

Smiling faintly good as gold
But over twenty decades old
Rabbits' ears may hear him play
But none will see him in the day
Owls' eyes see in the dark
His life ending in a final bark.

Danielle Frisby (12)
Loughborough High School

LAST CHANCE

Darkness descended on the world,
Like a huge heavy curtain,
Covering all life in its suffocating wrath.
People choking, screaming, dying,
In a lightless universe.
There was silence,
For the first time in countless millennia there was silence.

Time passed like the flapping of a hummingbird's wings,
Nothing to determine years from seconds.
Then there was Light,
Tumbling, swirling, like shards of coloured glass,
Fighting against Darkness' icy grip,
And then the evil reign was over.

Slowly, very slowly, life began to emerge.
A tiny flower opens,
Turning its face to the resurgent sun.
Suddenly, everywhere, huge explosions of colour burst out of nothing.
Life when once was void.

Years passed,
Stars formed and died.
Evolution took its extraordinary course.
The human race was given its final chance.

Johanna Kirby (13)
Loughborough High School

KALEIDOSCOPE

I was a child when I first saw,
The pretty patterns in bright colours;
And I heard the shaking prattle,
That sounded like a baby's rattle.

As people age they mature and develop,
Just like the shapes, that start as individuals,
But grow to be merged,
With other colours, patterns, people's lives.

The lives that change,
As do the pictures,
And colours that overlap and blend;
Where does variation ever end?

The cycles finish and do full circle,
Like fashions, friendships, life and luck;
There are the depressed and lonesome moments,
Though soon the fortune and contentedness fall.

So can you see, that when you're young,
You look through the hole and regard life's twisting routes;
But where will life's dance and fortune take you?
It's unpredictable, one does not know.

Life is like a spinning kaleidoscope.

Bryony Henderson Smith (14)
Loughborough High School

KALEIDOSCOPE

I feel I can control the world,
the hand that turns the wheel,
the one that changes the way things look,
the liberty is mine.

I see the grass and flowers grow,
the shapes take on a form,
they're mine, I created them,
the liberty is mine.

I see leaves and plants drop dead,
the beauty shrivels up,
I see my hand, I turn the wheel,
the liberty is mine.

I see the people of the world,
who hurry on their way,
I change the way their lives look,
from night to following day.

But then one day an image sticks,
and spins beyond control,
I cannot change that image now,
that liberty's not mine.

I cannot change the way it is,
or how the pattern looks,
but I can help it on its way,
that liberty is mine.

Frances Turner (14)
Loughborough High School

KALEIDOSCOPE

'It was always with you,'
My parents both said.
'You loved it so much,
You took it to bed.'
I remember the dreams,
I had with you;
We'd save people in fires,
We'd find lands a-new;
I would take you to school,
For show and tell,
But before it was my turn,
Off went the bell.
I never had a pet,
But I didn't really care;
I liked it better just you and me.
When no one else was there.
As I grew up,
And moved on in my life,
You were always with me,
Through trouble and strife.

From all this,
You can see,
Kaleidoscopes are a necessity.
When in trouble,
Or in doubt,
Look through the kaleidoscope
To help you out.

Zahra Sayar (13)
Loughborough High School

CALENDULA

A seed descends from its predecessor.
The progeny penetrates into the saturated soil.
It is nourished by the rain.
A minute green stem writhes its way to the surface.
Protruding leaves envelope the stalk.
A yellow and green patchwork bud resembles a crown.
Luminous yellow petals ease their way from their velvet folds.
The bloom flowers in all its magnificence until the dying
                                        of the late summer.
The bloom commences to fade,
Dropping its tarnished garments in mounds before it.
The menacing, malevolent frost bites the withering heads.
Nothing visible is left telling of the splendour of the
                                        once magnificent creation.
Winter has taken hold.
As the kaleidoscopic year spins around
Spring returns.
No reminiscence of the lifeless plant remains.
The recreated seed begins again to germinate.
The carousel is complete.

Imogen Mitchell (11)
Loughborough High School

THE ROLLER-COASTER

I'm going on a roller-coaster,
I'm waiting in the line,
I'm feeling very worried,
But Mum thinks it is fine.

My younger sister's ecstatic,
My mind is all a whirl,
This ride is too dramatic,
For a little girl.

I'm going to the start now,
I've lost all my ice-cream,
I think that any minute,
I am going to scream.

'Come on, let's go' my mummy said,
I looked at all the men,
'No way,' I said, 'that was fun,
I'm going on again.'

Charlotte Aldworth (11)
Loughborough High School

KALEIDOSCOPE

Butterflies twisting and turning upside down,
Look like the little sequins going round and round,
Twist the tube, turn the tube, round in many ways,
Making all the colours blur, into lots of funny shapes.

There are many colours, like red and blue,
Which remind me of peacocks, butterflies too,
The patterns are symmetrical and repeated four times,
You twist and it changes,
Then, sequins fall all around,
Like a butterfly as it flutters to the ground,
Optical shapes, patterns like stained glass windows,
Are seen, as well.

Kaleidoscopes, kaleidoscope circling around and round,
Making artistic and geometrical shapes all of the time.
Pretty colours, wonderful colours, colours like gems.
Are all memories of my favourite kaleidoscope, when I was ten.

Marsali MacGregor (14)
Loughborough High School

ODE TO A TOAD

The gorgeous English 'summer',
The rain, the sleet, the snow,
Mother really couldn't fathom,
Why her courgettes wouldn't grow.

She donned her shiny wellies,
Her anorak, her cag,
Strode out into the garden,
To visit her growbag.

She watered for a while,
Then stopped,
What was it she had seen?
What was it that was troubling our horticultural queen?

From beneath the orange plastic,
A rustling sound, she heard,
Was it something in the compost
She'd unwittingly disturbed?

The dog's *'What's this then?'* nose came down,
Stuck rigid to the bag,
From between a pair of furry legs,
A tail began to wag.

A crumpling sound of plastic,
A damp and earthy smell,
A little shower of compost,
Flicked up and slowly fell.

First a pair of goggle eyes,
Rose up out of the earth,
Then a clammy figure,
Hopped out onto the turf.

His feet were webbed and soily,
His skin was warty, brown,
Upon his knobbly little head,
He wore a chick-weed crown.

From that day on he's been there,
His peaceful life bestowed,
He's a stylish sort of fellow,
We call him Growbag Toad.

Alexy Karenowska (13)
Loughborough High School

KALEIDOSCOPE

Round and round,
The kaleidoscope turns.
Rapid and quick,
The kaleidoscope turns.
Black to white,
All different colours,
The kaleidoscope turns.
All in a hurry, all in a flurry,
Moving, spinning,
The kaleidoscope turns.
All individual,
Each one distinct,
The kaleidoscope turns.
Each on a mission,
Round and round,
The kaleidoscope turns.
One day it will stop,
All will unite,
And the kaleidoscope will no longer turn.

Faye Marriott (14)
Loughborough High School

THE CHAIR

Once upon a time I stood over there,
A beautiful, innocent mahogany chair.
People used to stand and stare
At me - I was 'wonderful'! 'Extraordinaire'!
They'd ask my keeper 'Oh, Mildred! Where
Did you get that delightful chair?'
They'd all praise my beauty fair,
And sometimes sit on me, if they dare.
Then my keeper bought another chair
Just like me - we were a pair!
So when people came up the stairs
They'd cry - 'Oh! *Two* delightful chairs!'
But then one day, it wasn't fair,
I was taken away - 'twas more than I could bear
A man came in, he had dark brown hair,
And his grating voice gave me quite a scare.
He took me away - I don't know where,
But wherever that place is, I'm still there.
Because nobody seems to care
About a once beautiful mahogany chair.

Kate Oatley (14)
Loughborough High School

THE KALEIDOSCOPE

Yellow leaves fall to the ground,
Down they fall without a sound.
From branches high on trees so tall,
A brown thrush sits sounding his call.
The air gets colder as the autumn breeze,
Goes under the hedge and over the trees.
But the seasons are changing and winter awaits.

Snow crunches under feet,
Dark branches covered in sleet.
Icicles shining in the mist,
Down the hillside the frozen streams twist.
Ice crystals like stars in the sky,
Snow coloured geese in the distance cry.
But the seasons are changing and springtime awaits.

Buds burst into colourful arrays,
And the young animals rejoice in their own ways.
Light green, diamond leaves appear,
And fox cubs adventure without any fear.
Woods full of bluebells, a mass of bright blue,
The pond full of frogspawn all life seems so new.
But the seasons are changing and summer awaits.

The sun bathes the land in light,
The longer the day the shorter the night.
The bee hums, the bird sings,
The butterfly flies and beats his wings.
The white roses climbing over the hedge,
The duck at the shining water's edge.
But the kaleidoscope is moving on, summer clouds fade
                    and autumn has begun.

Elizabeth Walley (12)
Loughborough High School

SIMPLY LIVING

How can this new feeling evoke such a sense of certainty within me?
Surely I have never felt this safe before?
Is it right that we should have so little, yet, have so much?
All around us people are fulfilling their dreams,
But we are simply living.

The complications of the civilised world all around us,
Is it fair that we are the only ones to ignore it?
We rely on no one, yet they all rely on us,
For how much longer will we be able to hide the
                              responsibilities that we have?
For we are simply living.

We can act, but in reality we lie in our hearts,
For we know that soon everything will be simple,
For us, the world and everything in it,
Will be a mantle in the eyes of you and me,
For we are simply living.

The human world looks at us with an eye of resent,
Have they never seen others like us?
If it occurs, then we will cause the greatest tragedy they ever knew,
They depend on us,
But we are simply living.

When we go, for we all have to,
We will be figures of the imagination,
Forgotten sympathies, memories, futures,
What will remain to represent us?
For we are simply dying.

Lydia Rose (12)
Loughborough High School

THE PRESENT

Positioned under the Christmas tree, lay a small crimson package,
Its rectangular shape was topped with a golden bow,
I stared at it unthinkingly,
Not long to go.

Christmas Day arrived at last,
My fingers moved nimbly, as the paper fell away,
Inside lay a small, silver tube glistening in the light,
Just what I wanted on this special day.

A multitude of colours was opened to my eyes,
As I tentatively held the object to the light,
I couldn't contain my surprise,
The colours so clear and bright.

Scarlet, cerulean and every other colour
A whirlwind of images and all to my eye.
What an amazing little instrument
How lucky am I!

Pattern after pattern of symmetry appears,
As if the rainbow is rotating,
The reds of autumn, the blues of winter, the green of spring and the
Yellow of summer all before me,
What a wonderful feeling.

'Hey! Put down my kaleidoscope' my sister's voice cut through,
My surprise was unbearable but a nod from my mother confirmed it,
I lowered the glistening silver tube back to its crimson box,
Oh well, at least I had a glimpse of a kaleidoscope.

Charlotte Day (12)
Loughborough High School

KALEIDOSCOPE

Today I found myself
In a world of many colours.
One which I had not seen before,
But was eager to explore.

I felt like I was looking
At a rainbow in the sky
Full of fiery colours
Which seemed almost unreal.

Like a rainbow that you cannot reach,
Like the pot of gold that can't be found,
Where the colours are intangible,
Untouchable to me.

I reach out to touch a colour
And before my eyes it changes
The tones and shapes slide and glide
To create a different pattern.

I am shocked by the brightness
Of the colours as they turn
Like the palette of a painter
Or the bright light of the sun.

I love the glaring, flaring colours
Of this unreal child's secret place
Now I have to leave my world of colour
And return to one that's dull.

Elizabeth Simpson (13)
Loughborough High School

KALEIDOSCOPE

Shattered images collide together like a joyful explosion,
Painting shapes in exotic colours that fill the screen.
A complex pattern falls into shape,
Like an autumn leaf, dotted with colour.
All the shades of brown, yellow and orange rush together,
Creating an autumn wave.

I reach out to grab this richness of colour,
But alas! This palette is guarded by a thick layer of glass.
No one can destroy it.
Suddenly I lose control, the picture is gone,
For all now I look upon is a blurred image of a rainbow.

I have not lost all, for I turn the kaleidoscope,
And to my joy and surprise find another picture waiting before me.
This time wild colours of black, yellow and red clash together
                                    in a furious battle.
As if it was spring, every colour awaits to be let out for a new start.
Every colour dances across the screen to unleash yet more visions.

Like a book, each image unfolds its own story.
Pixies dance in green, begging you to join them,
Whilst colder colours splinter into icy daggers,
That burst into a joyful spray of colours.

Joanna Jaroszkiewicz (13)
Loughborough High School

KALEIDOSCOPE

The seasons whirl around and round,
Full of colours and of sound,
Like the shapes inside the toy,
Which bring many children joy.

Spring brings colours new and young,
An azure sky and an amber sun,
Fresh green grass and flowers bright,
All make spring a season of light.

Showy, luscious and vivid colour,
Is the sign of a brilliant summer,
A scarlet sky and a green lawn,
A gilt frame surrounding a field of corn.

Autumn brings colours of fawn and beige,
The leaves on the trees showing their age,
Crisp grey mornings and a sandy sky,
All tell people that autumn is nigh.

Winter, dingy, dismal and grey,
Brings with it the snow in which children play,
Dull, dreary mornings and dark, black nights,
Are all drab and dowdy sights.

The kaleidoscope of nature,
From spring until winter,
The shapes inside God's toy,
Which brings the world so much joy.

Donna Pilcher (13)
Loughborough High School

KALEIDOSCOPE

Twisting and changing,
Changing and twisting,
Round and round again,
Like life in an ever-turning wheel,
Around it turns again.
First comes the merry colour of red,
Who brightens up our day,
As a burning ball of fire,
It floats around the sky.
Then is the peaceful colour of blue,
Who laps upon the shore,
But the mood changes every day,
From dark straight through to light.
The kindest colour I must admit,
Is the joyful colour of green,
It dances in the luscious fields,
In which the children play.
My favourite colour is definitely,
A mix of blue and red,
Sometimes it can be very calm
Other times it is mad.
When mixed together, those colours create,
The colours of our world,
Without them here, our world would be,
A pretty boring place.
Twisting and changing,
Changing and twisting,
Round and round again,
Like in an ever-turning wheel,
Around it turns again.

Jeni McNicoll (14)
Loughborough High School

KALEIDOSCOPE

Red, orange, pink and green,
coloured glass gems,
yellow, peach, purple and blue,
reflecting mosaics ever-changing.
All sparkling and gleaming,
like a well polished floor.
Rotate the end,
listen, hear the harsh sound,
of rice in a jar.
Picture chicks, trees and five pandas' faces,
watch flowers explode,
like a building on fire.
Stars and diamonds,
hexagons and octagons,
all encircled,
within my kaleidoscope.

Alexandra Campbell (14)
Loughborough High School

KALEIDOSCOPE

I picture something, a hope, a dream,
All arranged, every piece like I want it to be.
Different pieces make up my dream.
Each representing a different angle to look at it,
A different view or opinion.
I decide my dream, I can see each piece slotting into place.
It's bright, new and captivating,
A rainbow of different colours,
Each one reflecting another,
Hope reflecting joy, sadness reflecting hope.

Each angular face, circular place,
Seem to fit together perfectly.
I get lulled into a false sense of happiness.
I can see my plans, my dreams and plans,
Changing in front of me.
The sections swirling round and round.
I think all is lost.
Until I look again down my tunnel of dreams.
I see a new hope, a fresh start.

Claire Cunliffe (14)
Loughborough High School

KALEIDOSCOPE

India, China, Africa, Japan,
Each has its own type of man,
But all should have an equal right,
To live freely and in delight.
Jamaica, England and Pakistan,
All should be able to do what they can,
To make this world a better place,
Irrelevant of colour or race.
People have unique colour and style,
Just like the numbers on a dial,
Choose a friend by personality,
Regardless of their nationality.
Europe, Asia and Germany,
It doesn't matter much to me,
We should put the world together again,
With all the different religions of men.
All together we could still cope,
Like one great big kaleidoscope!

Rebecca Johnson (14)
Loughborough High School

KALEIDOSCOPE

A robin sings his morning song,
Children wake,
Excited to see
Their stockings full of goodies.
A child grabs her sack
And runs into her parents' room,
Where she pulls out a long,
Tube shaped present.

Quickly she rips it open,
Out falls a kaleidoscope,
She lifts it up to her eye
And closing the other, looks through.
The hypnotising colours twist and turn
To make new shapes and patterns,
She looks into a new life,
A life that's always changing.

She twists the tubes,
Making the shapes collide and merge,
Forming a new fashion, a style,
Then she moves on again.
She leaves school and travels,
As colours mix and lives change,
She settles down and gets a job,
Gets married and has kids.

But the colours kept changing,
She takes the kaleidoscope
And puts it back in the box,
As she remembers the good times, long ago.

Helen Alderson (14)
Loughborough High School

DARKNESS

Day has fallen into the pit at the end of the world,
Darkness looms,
Stars scattered,
Flicked into the sky by a giant hand.
Silence.
All you can hear is the sound of the wind rustling the trees in its path.
Suddenly a car whizzes past, shattering the silence
into small, broken pieces.
You wait for the silence to rebuild itself.
All is dark and mysterious.
Illuminated only by the street lamps, piercing the ground
with spears of light.
Again, silence is broken by the pitter-patter of rain,
Drumming against the window pane.
You tug the curtain open and see a poor spider trying to spin its web.
You are about to close the curtain and a flash of lightning
cracks the sky.
Thunder follows, shaking the earth with its power and control.
The wind beats the trees with wickedness,
Like a teacher caning them for wrong doing.
Rain drums harder on the window pane,
And you see the spider being whisked away in the wind.
Outside all is havoc.
You gradually hear the thunder getting softer,
The rain becomes quieter,
The wind starts to say it's sorry,
And the silence rebuilds itself.
You see the sun rising, pulling itself from the pit.
You see the spider climbing back up the wall,
Ready to start her work again.
Then the street busies,
The silence has been smashed once more,
But there's always tonight!

Helen Bailey (12)
Loughborough High School

Trapped In A Corner Of A Kaleidoscope

We laugh and shout,
It's a normal day,
Nothing gets in our way.
But do we know how much we'll damage?
How much land we're going to savage?

The trees fall,
The oceans thin,
Money starts pouring in.
But money can't buy us the life we need,
Money can't rescue us from the clutches of greed.

Everything is fine,
It's like a dream,
How brightly the money seems to gleam!
Life is great but how long for?
Maybe the end is already knocking on our door.

Death has been let in,
We start to die,
People also start to cry.
We can't do anything, we've swallowed the bait,
There is nothing to do, we're far too late.

We try to save, but nature has gone,
We treated it too often as a simple minority,
Money won on our list of priorities.
We've realised our mistakes,
But there is no hope,
We are still trapped in a corner of a kaleidoscope.

We had a chance,
We never saw it,
Stuck in a corner of a kaleidoscope.

Lucia Li (12)
Loughborough High School

KALEIDOSCOPE

Colours swirling around and around,
Pictures floating up and down.
Shapes bouncing, bouncing all around,
Patterns forming everywhere.

Seeing patterns forming,
Forming to make a memory.
Making me remember,
The good times and the bad.

Here I am sitting all forlorn,
Thinking of what I might be doing,
As if I were in the past,
In the same situation.

I might be swimming,
In my best friend's pool.
Or I might be running,
Down the old running track.

I used to sit back relaxing,
Until my friend would come along.
Then we used to run out screaming,
To be long, long gone.

When I was eight I remember a holiday,
Where we (the whole family) went to Frith.
Then it snowed and we played until night,
Only to be forgotten when we were out of sight.

That was my childhood,
Once long forgotten.
Only to be revived,
By the old kaleidoscope.

Kathryn Mallett (11)
Loughborough High School

THE WAY THROUGH SANITY

They shut the home where the 'insane' stayed
Seven years ago.
The men in suits have undone it again,
And now you would never know
There was a home seven years ago
Before they built those walls and bars.
It is underneath those sad, pale faces
The sparks of their personalities,
Only the doctor sees
Their individuality
Once trapped in the home
They shut the home where the 'insane' stayed.
Now, if you go into the homes
Of the people with sad, pale faces
The homes of the 'fools' are filled with
Jewels of laughter,
They sit with mates
(They fear not the medication and the men in white coats
because they see so few)
You can see the ambition
And plans for the future
Evolving and developing
Through the normality of life,
As though they perfectly knew
That the bricks and bars were gone
There is now no home for the 'insane'.

Anita Chaggar (12)
Loughborough High School

KALEIDOSCOPE

Life is like a kaleidoscope,
The picture never stays the same.
The shapes turning and spinning,
A complex explosion of fame.

Watch the plastic rise and fall,
Watch the reflections on the mirrors.
Look at the patterns, irregular change,
Look at the different colours.

The rainbow of surprise is never the same,
More broken pictures round each curve.
The twisting freedom of the shapes,
Watch them dodge and swerve.

Keep gazing down that tube,
Gazing into the dreams.
Look at exploding fireworks,
Nothing is what it seems.

The art, no artists could draw,
Is staring you in the face.
There's a swirling rainbow of colour,
You're not staring into space.

You look away, out of the light,
It all becomes dark.
It's the end of your life,
It's the end of the art.

Jennifer Creaser (13)
Loughborough High School

KALEIDOSCOPE

The curious, coloured tube,
Could this actually
Be what the others said -
Right now I cannot see.

I really, really want to know,
Just one way to find out.
As soon as I just peep inside,
Inside me there's no doubt.

Soft, gentle colours,
Yellow, green and red,
Wind in the meadows,
Gorgeous flower bed.

Just a handy twist,
Pink, purple and blue.
Magic in the sky,
Clouds of every hue.

Just two simple ones,
Classic black and white,
A frosty winter morning,
The dark sky at night.

Wondrous and striking,
Magenta, turquoise, teal.
Exploring in the rainforest,
With amazing zeal.

These colours melt away,
I can't always be here,
I now return kaleidoscope,
Still keeping it quite near.

Lei Wang (12)
Loughborough High School

FRIENDSHIP - WAR

One dark autumn day,
The wind was howling like a ghost
The sun had not risen from its nest,
And Mary had just received her post.

A letter from her friend in Sweden,
Darkened her day even more
She had already feared the worst,
Now their countries were at war.

The hatred, the anger, the sorrow
Flooded her mind,
Things won't be the same,
War was not a game.

Darkness, darkness finishes the
Day, darkness.

The bombs had started,
The war had begun
Sorrow and despair
Was everywhere.

Darkness, darkness finishes the
Month, darkness.

Ring, ring, the phone was calling,
Susan her friend was crying out loud.
Then a bang; the phone was cut off,
A bomb sent out a big, black cloud.

Darkness, darkness ended her life.

Darkness, darkness filled the air,
Darkness, darkness everywhere.

Jackie Upton (12)
Loughborough High School

INSIDE A GIRL'S HEAD

Inside an aeroplane
soaring across the world.
Pen in my hand
note book on my leg.
White trees,
holly leaves,
icicles hanging from eaves.
These things go round my head,
when I'm tucked up in bed.

Locked in a library,
stuck in my own world,
head in a book,
carried to a magical land.
Friends around me,
laughing happily,
singing gaily.
These things go round my head,
when I'm tucked up in bed.

Brothers bothering me,
following and pestering me,
putting spiders in my bed,
and sniggering behind me.
Laughing craftily,
pointing daftly.
What have they done now?
These things go round my head,
when I'm tucked up in bed.

Anna Krarup (12)
Loughborough High School

KALEIDOSCOPE

Kaleidoscope surrounded by patterns and colours,
as I walk inside it reminds me of lovers
at first they're packed together
then they're spread apart
it doesn't always go like this
it depends on the heart.

Kaleidoscope it's my beautiful world
the shape they make
how they bend and curl.
Round and round and round it swirled
I treasured it as if it was a precious pearl.

Kaleidoscope is such a magical thing
shake it about and you'll hear it cling,
different sizes big and small
it's my favourite toy, and most of all
it's my kaleidoscope.

I love my kaleidoscope I really do,
when I need it, it helps me see through,
see through my problems and my anger inside,
my kaleidoscope is the best thing since dignity and pride.

Rebecca Culver (14)
Rawlins Community College

CARING FOR HORSES ABROAD

Working down dirty, dusty lanes,
being whacked with big, hard canes.
What's it like in the real world?
I don't know because I've never been in the real world.
They are poor, but so am I,
I might as well just cry.
All over my body there are scars, bruises and cuts,
I pray to God that some day it stops.
Life is a big thing to cope with,
I am still here to live.
All this is for is money,
They don't have the time to look at me and see,
I could be beautiful and lovely.

Amy Garner (13)
Redmoor High School

THE CHAIR OF CHICKEN WIRE

The chair has four wire legs which are flimsy and old.
It has a feeble and shiny frame.
Holding the laddered, rough chicken wire seat.
The seat looks saggy and old.
Unwilling to support any weight at all.
The rotting and dissolving seat.
Which looks like it will break any minute.
The chair has different attributes; in places it is soft,
While others it is rough, rugged and sharp.

Trevor Bell (16)
The Rutland College

DAD

I don't remember you,
But I'm told you were there.
Why did you leave so soon?
Didn't you care?

I don't get upset.
Why should I cry?
It was your decision,
And you chose to die.

I can never forgive you,
For what you have done.
Why weren't you there,
When I needed someone?

I often wonder,
How my life would be,
If you hadn't died,
If you'd stayed with me.

If you'd stayed around,
You could have watched me grow,
Protected me from all that's bad,
And taught me all you know.

I will never know you,
And I just can not hide,
This empty feeling,
That's always inside.

If only I could talk to you,
Then you could let me know,
If I was the reason,
You felt you had to go.

Zoë Berry (16)
The Rutland College

THE PRIZE

Before they caught the scent I
felt it
I realised running
fear was the ghost enveloping me

Close enough to the jaws
of the hungry
snapping
Their cry is ancient
My fear is now

I am running hard,
My master makes me chase that
are my cousins and
Is the prize worth
the price?

Who is there to help me
escape a fate that
should not be
mine?

My legs grow weaker
I feel their greedy breath
greed
Driving for the prize

The time is near
I feel it
I've forgotten I am running
Triumph is the ghost enveloping me

I feel the tide turn
The distance grows!
But the huntsman raises his whip against
the laws and rights of nature

And the fox falls
I hear an ancient cry
The prize is now mine
And the price is
forgotten.

Emma Chivers (17)
The Rutland College

A FADING MEMORY

The sweet smelling scent,
I could taste as you left.
The memories flood back,
Which I can never forget.

The touch of your hand,
Gives a warm feeling within,
My heart starts to race,
As I remembered your face.

The good times we shared,
Weigh out all the bad.
The tears ever flowing,
After all that we had.

Your kindness caressed me,
Your warmness possessed me.
The promise you kept,
That you'll never forget.

The memory will never fade,
As I look back on the old,
The love that we made,
Will never unfold.

Sally Sturgess (16)
The Rutland College

A MODERN FAMILY

The first born, Mum says never again.
My parents, a young and inexperienced couple.
I had all the attention,
I was the first child, grandchild,
And niece.

Two years later, my parents had decided,
What I needed was someone to grow up with,
But I was blessed,
My parents reassure me, that twins are
Better than one.

My life changed, three to four years later,
On the surface a very happy family, no problems
Or so I thought.
My dad decided to leave with a gentle push, and live
On a boat.

It didn't take long, eight months to a year,
Another woman and her newly born son - Stepfamily,
Who would have thought.
A new addition, my first half brother. It didn't
Stop there. Oh no.

I'm glad it didn't stop there, for my mum's sake.
She too met a guy and remarried, those too had a baby,
Another half brother for me.
Back to my father, to make my family complete,
Latest addition, a girl.

A modern family forget 2.4 children expand,
Have seven.

Clare Connors (16)
The Rutland College

PINK AND PURPLE

Open toed, black velvet,
Skipping and skittering - head in the clouds.
Pink and purple blurring together
Whirling round in a Jaffa Cake packet.

Pink on the inside, full of fun,
Bubbling over and up to the sparkle -
in her eyes
Slightly Welsh, sleep talking mumblations
ohmastik where are you going - thinking?
I don't know.

Running and tripping, forgetting.
Go back to the beginning. I said 'Go!'
Never listens - only to the steamy baguettes and car windows.
Responsive to my feelings - 'Are you alright? Are you sure?'
Free calls all over the place waking me up,
And *that* saying 'You lie baby'!
Well, that's her for you.

Lucy Riches (16)
The Rutland College

WATERFALL ON FOUR SKINNY LEGS . . .

It stands unevenly on 4 skinny legs,
With a white straight back,
Slightly rough but at the same time smooth to touch,
The shape of the chair is like a waterfall with a straight drop
                                    into the lake,
Slowly it runs down bumpily as slight waves.

Paula Brown (15)
The Rutland College

MEMORIES

Every memory close to my heart
Is a page in the book of life
From good and bad times
To all my hopes and dreams.

Looking back through the book
I now see the changes I have made
Be they right or wrong
Each affecting me in a different way.

Knowing if I'd made different decisions
I wouldn't be the person I am now
So the question is
Did I make the right ones?

I will never know the answer
But every page is a different stage
Helping me now,
To fulfil my every dream.

Emma Keogh (16)
The Rutland College

A PIECE OF ART

The chair is small.
A piece of art,
It's dull and white, it's fragile and light.
It stands uneven on its wire legs,
It appears to have a rough, sharp edge.
Unstable, unsafe, yet a valuable piece of art.

Rachel Sam Veasey (17)
The Rutland College

MYSELF THE CONTRADICTION

I'm in a group on my own
I'm rich but I'm poor
I was homeless with a home
I'm interesting but a bore
Honest yet deceitful
Confident yet nervous
I'm uplifting while depressing
Intelligent yet slow
Complex only simple
Young but I feel old
Puerile while mature
I'm reality in a fantasy
I'm myself but not to you.

Thom Wilson (16)
The Rutland College

SITTING PRETTY?

The chair is small.
The chair is white.
Still it seems quite all right.
It has three legs supporting and one, which is not.
The legs look like fingers trying to cross.
After I looked closer I could see,
That it was full of holes and seemed fragile.
The chair looks tired, like a veteran of war.
The chair after being touched is sharp edged, rough and flexible.
And in the wrong hands could be dangerous.
Is it still 'sitting pretty'?

Andrew Bewick (18)
The Rutland College

MISSING YOU

I have visions of your face in my mind,
It stands out as clear as the brightest star,
In this space love we will find,
Even though you are so far.

The plans we have promised are all still there,
One day we will be back together as one,
Look after my heart and please take care,
Our life together has just begun.

When I remember those days, I sit and smile,
I hope the memories are dear to you too,
The distance between us is more than a mile,
I just need you to know, that I'll always love you.

Laura Grey (17)
The Rutland College

OVER THE AGES

Standing in the middle, unique and lonely,
Overlooked by the people,
Too fragile for mankind.

Years of children's tea parties
Gives a feeling of uncare with its legs bent and unstable,
With a seat like lapping waves, uneven and worn.

Sandra Deal (17)
The Rutland College

ORIGINS

Where are you from?
Most people will ask
when you meet them.
But what do you say if you don't know?

Born in a foreign country,
brought up there
and learnt their language,
went to school
and made friends there,
but not expected to call it home.

But now sitting in a country she hardly knows,
has learnt their language,
but hasn't got many friends,
only relatives.
How come she can call this home?

When she was there,
she would say she was from here.
But now she is here,
she says she is from there.

So where is she from?
From here or there?
But does she have to decide?
Can't she be from here and there?

Helen Roberts (16)
The Rutland College

A Tribute To My Grandad

He was the man who'd sit in his chair smoking old Park Drive,
He was the man, who looked after me,
He was the man, who I sat and watched slowly growing old,

He was the man, who'd always have time to play cards or dominoes,
He was the man, who cuddled me when I cried or was sad and afraid,
He was the man, who wiped away my tears,
He was the man, who looked after me when I was sick.

He was the man, who made me what he called special trifle,
                                              ones without custard,
He was the man, who took me to the shops and brought me
                              secret sweets, ones not to tell Nana about,
He was the man, who'd buy me ice-cream when it was hot,
He was the man, who'd cook us all Sunday lunch,

He was the man, who looked after me for 8 or more years after school,
He was the man, that came to all my school plays,

He was the man, who watched me grow into a happy teenager,
He was the man, who waited to hear my exam results at 16
                                              and was pleased,

These were the memories of the man I love,
But
He was much more than that to me, he was my Grandad!

Rebecca Potter (17)
The Rutland College

A JOURNEY OF A LIFETIME

From a single egg thus life begins
A creation from God disposed with sins
An innocent child
Obedient and sweet
Only to be spoiled by those they greet

As life proceeds the child matures
Developing thoughts you thought were yours
Primed and perceptive
Playful but smart
I just wish at times they played the part!

Adolescence creeps in to be welcomed by some
Adopting attitudes thus left undone
Accomplished and competent
Cunning and shrewd
Yet such a rebellion and oh so rude!

A responsible adult has now progressed
Embellishing now into one so stressed
Tired and fatigued
Lonely and debilitated
And presumed to do what everyone hated

A happy couple with now a child
Entering a world so fierce and wild
Tangible views
Mellow prospects
But living a life so full of regrets.

Adam Smith (16)
The Rutland College

HELP!

What does it mean to be 'normal'?
I search for someone to tell
Me the reason,
For this damned definition.

Why does no one understand?
My thoughts, my emotions, my fears and my dreams,
They point, they stare, create rumours and wonder.

I may have a problem
But still no one helps,
I'm lost and alone,
And see no way out.

James Waller (16)
The Rutland College

SLAVERY

'Faster, faster,' they scream.
We row so fast the strain is killing us.
The sun bakes down on us,
sending beads of sweat trickling down our foreheads.

Where are we going?
'To the civilised countries,
to work for the white men,
to whom you'll belong,' they say.

'Why should we belong to anyone?
We're not animals.'
I feel like screaming out.
But I must resist the urge
or suffer a beating.

The injustice of our situation is intolerable.
Surely God made everyone equal?

Obviously he forgot about us.

Hannah Taylor (16)
The Rutland College

IMMORTAL COLOURS

I started as a blank page, wafer thin, light as air,
That same page now in a mass of raging colours,
There are no perfect pictures, just the swirls of emotions.
All the colours you can imagine are there, on that page that is my life.
I dare you to look, look deeply into my eyes,
Peer through the clouds and deep into my soul,
What you see is changing all the time,
Those thoughts that pass, those emotions that run through my body,
All are caught, dragged in and exploded outwards to be scattered.
Never will you be able to catch a lasting memory of what you find,
As though when you draw back away from soul,
Out through the clouds and into the air that you hope to breath,
Your mind is swept clean.
You are left alone with only a chance glimpse of what passed,
But when you see a twinkle, through the doors which
                              once you searched,
You may still see the colours mix in turmoil, as warm life
                              flows through my body.

Vicky Ellis (16)
The Rutland College

HOPE

It's time for bed,
the weasel said

as the snow came falling down.
It plastered a snow-white layer,

on the rough uneven ground.
The hibernating hedgehogs,

sleep cuddled in their leaves.
A world so unconnected,

seems invisible to thieves.

An owl cries out a warning,
a fox screams in the night.

The snowflakes keep on falling,
to cover all the plight.

A few miles to the south,
a view so torrid lies,

of chimney smoke and buildings,
of corruption and of bribe.

A murder, a minute hitman,
prowls the lonely streets.

Stalking a naive victim,
like a copper on the beat.

Scared people twitch the curtains,
a lookout on a post,

pleading ignorance to trouble,
away from those feared most.

In the stitching of a blanket,
corruption has not crept.

A tiny baby playing,
mother's tears rest wet.

Hope.

Kaye Houston (16)
The Rutland College

AN INCREDIBLE LOSS

I stand alone and perfectly still
Meanwhile this world is crumbling and falling around me
Only shouts and screams will now surround me
Some in excitement, many trembling with fear
For the hope is fading now the end is near.

Precious memories now cease to exist
Everything I once believed in drifts from my head
My future plans are extinguished and my dreams are dead
And all that remains are thoughts of terror and fear
For my little life seems pointless now the end is near.

The world is silent but the strain is showing,
The sky is falling and the heart is slowing,
The earth is trembling and the life is going.
Am I here alone now?

The light is fading and darkness takes control
But the stars are not shining and where is the moon?
I know it is coming, it will have to be soon
And my mind is empty but my heart is full of fear
For the end is not coming, the end is here.

Laura Plant (16)
The Rutland College

QUESTIONS OF LIFE

Why do children act so cruel
By torturing other kids at school?
Because they're insecure.

Why do multi-national corporations
Rape the starving nation?
Because of greed.

Why do people walk on by
The homeless man, ignoring his cry?
Because they're ignorant.

Why do people act so bitter
When they insist on dropping litter?
Because they're careless.

Why do nations prevent unity existing anymore
By fighting in a world war?
Because they're selfish.

Why do racists insult and holler
At people who are a different colour?
Because they're arrogant.

Why can't nature be set free
And society be allowed to live in harmony?
Because it's impossible.

Louisa Daniel (17)
The Rutland College

MUMMY, MUMMY . . .

'Mummy, Mummy' she asks as we sit down to eat,
'Why eat my greens, when I've eaten my meat?'

'Well do you want your pudding, please let me know!
If you eat all your greens you're guaranteed to grow!'

She sits in the nursery surrounded by toys,
'Mummy, Mummy what is the difference between girls and boys?'

'Well, the stork makes us different, blame the birds and the bees.
We all descended from apes who swing from the trees!'

We're stuck in a traffic jam, moving slowly on our way,
'Mummy, Mummy are we nearly there yet?' is the topic today.

'Sshh, I'm concentrating, be patient and wait,
All these disturbances are making us late!'

We're in the front room, decorating the pine tree,
'Mummy, Mummy how's Santa arriving when we haven't a chimney?'

'Don't panic my angel, be good and believe,
As you'll know in the morning from the gifts you receive!'

We're in the library talking to the receptionist lady,
'Mummy, Mummy where did I come from as a baby?'

By now this aggravation makes my face burn hot,
'Hang on darling . . . wait one second, I forgot!'

Melanie Finnemore (17)
The Rutland College

MANKIND

The rain which falls from above is all the tears
Earth has shed since mankind began

The thunder which fills the sky is a plea from Him
for mankind to stop tearing the world apart

The lightning is the anger He shares with us
to remind mankind to live in peace

The wind represents His power over mankind
reminding us of His great strength

The early morning sun warms the hearts of mankind
filling them with His love

Every new dawn brings with it a new beginning
for mankind.

Deborah Glancy (16)
The Rutland College

I WAS NOT WITH YOU

I remember us together,
My grandpa and I.
Playing together on holiday,
Every year, for four short years.
In Skegness, Hunstanton or Cromer.
You and I and Nanny too.

No one could imagine the times to come.
The cancer that never went away.
Doctors, drugs and nurses could not help.
So together we were left to face that fatal day.
You and I and Nanny too.

I was not with you on that day,
Something I deeply regret.
I was not with you on that day,
To say goodbye. So instead,
You sent your love, with Nanny,
Something that will never fade away.

Krystina Kinkade (16)
The Rutland College

POISON GROWTH

Words killing you
Slaps wounding you
Manipulation dragging you
Down.
Patronisation giving you
Inferiority.
Humiliation dividing you
Into 3, 4, 6 personas.
Poison is surrounding you
It grows
Someone passed it
On to you.
But it's not catching
It just grows and grows
Through generation to generation.
Inherited.
Will your children grow up
In your poison?

Julia Riley (16)
The Rutland College

ME

As I stand in the mirror,
What do I see?
A perfect picture,
Or a form of imagery?

All the features are there,
Blond hair, blue eyes,
But what I cannot see,
Are the things that lie inside.

My body's just a cover,
For all the things I feel,
Emotions, feelings,
Possessions people cannot steal.

I'd like to think I'm nice,
In lots of different ways,
But like any human being,
I also have bad days.

But these are things that only I possess,
Not to be swapped in any way,
I wouldn't change them for all the world,
Not even to be different for a single day.

Laura Orton (16)
The Rutland College

MY ROOM, MY MESS

My room's a mess, wet towels left lying,
Clothes and books up to the door,
Pieces of old bike scattered,
Homework crumpled and tattered
I can't even see the floor!
'Tidy your room' said my mother
'And please try and find your brother, he was last seen in here'
My brother's lost somewhere in my room.
Oh dear.

My room's a mess, where to begin?
Oh crikey, a flowery dress
Better put that in the bin!
What am I doing?
I've got no idea.
Mum's right about one thing
I've got some funny gear,
A giant yellow fish,
A statue of Elvis,
Oh and a decorative dish.

My room's no longer a mess, I've tidied up!
Books and clothes pushed under the bed
Along with a big hairy bug, which was dead.
Mum will be pleased though, I found a coffee mug
And a pot of green Flubber, but alas,
I still didn't find my little brother.

Richard Chisholm (16)
The Rutland College

IF THE WORLD ENDED TOMORROW . . .

If the world ended tomorrow
There would be:
No more suffering souls,
Pollution would be no more
But at what cost?
No more animals to change with evolution,
No more wars,
No more prejudice,
No more racism,
No more wrong and no more right,
No more new technology,
No more new lives,
No more me and you,
And no more you and me,
But if the world ended tomorrow
Who would finish the Millennium Dome?

Alexa Kenny (16)
The Rutland College

THE FIRST THOUGHT

The most sophisticated product of evolution
Earth has become our slave
Its purpose to assure our survival
Main objective of all living things

Forever ascending the staircase of efficiency
Each step discarded once used
All knowing a line should be drawn
Yet the pen is passed through each generation
Running out of ink after a fraction of completion

We are beyond the struggle for survival
Time for the first thought to be made
A new agenda set
Before endless resources run out
And our main objective cannot be met.

Jonathan Bird (16)
The Rutland College

UNTITLED

Throw it at me,
Paint me with it,
Fill and overflow me
                with it,
But when I grow up,
I want to be me.

Shout it at me,
Wash me with it,
Inject and drug me up
                with it,
But when I grow up,
I want to be me.

Don't dress me,
Don't mess me,
Don't make me or break me,
You won't change
                or derange me,
Because when I grow up,
I'm going to me.

Emily Moss (17)
The Rutland College

DEAR GEORGE

As the old chest creeks open
I am overcome by emotions
as I remember the times we shared
you were my pillar of strength
through the good times
and the bad
I pick out your diary and blow off the dust
the pages old and frail
show the now faded marks of your writing
my eyes fill with tears as I recall you
sitting at your desk
writing these very words
all those years ago.
Peering into the old chest once again
I see a small bundle of pictures
tied with some delicate ribbon
I unfasten the ribbon and hold the pictures close to my heart
remembering.
The photographs though faded
are still reminiscent of your tender face
the face that will never be replaced or forgotten
in all my days.
Although I have this old chest
filled to the brim with your belongings
overflowing with memories of you
I tell myself
it is not the materialistic objects that matter
for the memories I hold dearest
will be locked away forever
not in an old chest
but in my heart.

Siân Penfold (17)
The Rutland College

ONLY AN OPINION

When does space end?
It plays on my mind as nobody knows,
Or can find out the answer.
Does it end?
Maybe it doesn't.
No.
Surely it does.

Who made the rule that we are alone,
In this vast amount of space that surrounds us?
'Extra terrestrial life, ha, no way!'
Why not?
Maybe we are not oh so superior.

What is it like to be born?
We have all experienced it,
But none of us know.
Perhaps we are programmed to forget,
What has no further meaning to us,
As life begins there.

Why give us life,
Only to take it away from us again?
Does our mind live on?
If it doesn't, then surely
There is a purpose in life.
A mission to complete,
A discovery to me made.
A question to be answered.

Alan Lloyd (18)
The Rutland College

SECOND CHANCE

Gazing from a moonlit star
at the world beneath my feet
helpless!
I see no means of return
to a world that was home not so long ago

If only I had a second chance
I wouldn't be so frivolous
I'd treasure life, it's a precious belonging
like the home that I had not so long ago

Reincarnation!
That's the ticket
on cloud nine I'd travel back
to a home that I once worshipped
a home that was mine not so long ago

Now I'm in a queue
but so far from the front where
the chief himself majestically sits
my second chance would be greatly used
on a world that was mine not so long ago

Time has aged me as I've waited so long
but finally my time has come
I see the way and the path is in sight
the path to my home that I left long ago.

Kathryn Walters (18)
The Rutland College

RUN

Bang!
Gun smoking
Everyone running
Heart pumping
Feet sweating
Eyes looking
Back glancing
Tension growing
Muscles aching
Shoes pounding
Tape approaching
Breath easing
All slowing
Faces glowing
Looking
Knowing
Skin cooling
Wondering
Waiting
He was cheating
Start again,
Bang!

Antonia Garnett-Clarke (17)
The Rutland College

DISTANCE

To be close to you,
To inject sweet sugar into my blood.

I see you in life's grand ballroom,
And I tremble to see you again.

And if tonight be our last,
May our love glow eternally, never a flicker.

She shows me heaven,
I could walk on water,

And if tomorrow makes us,
And if tomorrow breaks us,

Like a wave crashing into the shore,
You wash away my dreams.

Angus Hammond (17)
The Rutland College

THE FAT FLY

There was a fat fly,
Flew past my eye,
That I did spy.

I whacked at his wing,
A song he did sing,
His neck I could wring.

Charlotte Swift (11)
The Rutland College

An Evening In The Country

As the sun goes down through
        a pastel sky,
And the silhouettes of trees
        grow dark,
The screech owls deep in the woods
        do cry,
And the dogs at the farm
        they bark.
The crickets sing where the
        wild flowers grow,
And the stars in the sky
        switch on.
The lights in the windows of
        houses glow,
And to bed all young
        children have gone.

Holly Potter (12)
Uppingham Community College

Our Changing World!

All things changing in their own way
New things happen every day
Babies are born
The elderly die
But there's just one question I want answered
Why why why do we die?
To make way for the new generations
To make friends with other civilisations
The world is changing every day
Changing, changing in every way.

Katie Holroyd (12)
Uppingham Community College

THE ELECTRIC SHOCK

Earthquakes are unpredictable,
They are disruptive shocks.
They may occur immensely
Like a ten second electric shock.
Like a tiger's teeth tearing a carcass
As the buildings shudder and shake.
Eventually they retreat
Collapsing to the floor
Large cracks in the earth occur.
Feet deep they are
As black as ink.
Like a hollow cave,
Or like a dragon's cave.
Eventually the earthquake halts.
The earth is flat and dead.
Debris everywhere so dark and still
And *dead.*
Shock, shock, shock.

Joanna Millington (12)
Uppingham Community College

PHILOSOPHISING

The philosopher said to the mongoose,
'Why do you think we are here?
Is existence just something we can't understand -
Is the earth just a meaningless sphere?'

The mongoose replied rather idly,
'Yes the Earth is a meaningless ball,
And life's just a way that we live, my dear friend,
It isn't a puzzle at all!'

The philosopher paused and then answered:
'Then how is everything here?
Is it God? Is it science - or perhaps is it fate?
Our end. Is it far? Is it near?'

The mongoose became quite sarcastic and said:
'If I were like you - such a boff . . .
But I'm not and I won't be, you bore me to death,'
And he stretched out his legs and stalked off.

Rosie Forth (12)
Uppingham Community College

THE QUICK GAME

The small white man leads the team out,
would they lose really badly, hardly a doubt,
the team that were red started to warm up,
they must play really well to win the cup.

The big fat ref stood bold in the sun,
there was a rumour that he weighed a ton,
the silver whistle was in his sweaty hand,
both sides were ready to protect their land.

The front of the whistle entered his mouth,
the blue team were playing from north to south,
the echoing sound went over the grass,
the red team were ready to play the first pass.

The game had started the ball went right,
the floodlights were on, with their shining lights,
90 minutes had gone, time was up,
the winning team went up to lift the cup.

Joshua Walker (12)
Uppingham Community College

FIREWORKS AND BONFIRES

Fireworks lighten up the sky
Bonfires brighten up so high,
Lots of people gather round
To see the fireworks shoot from the ground.

Bonfires sparkle, sizzle and pop
Fireworks shoot up right to the top,
Circles of colours in the air
While people are talking
While people stare.

Fireworks, fireworks finishing soon
Bonfire smoke covers the moon,
All the people say 'Goodbye'
To the bonfires and fireworks that light up the sky.

Sonia Whitsey (11)
Uppingham Community College

FIREWORKS

F ire lights up the rocket
I n the street the sky lights up
R ockets shoot up and blow up the sky
E veryone looks anxiously into the sky
W eeping animals cry to get inside
O pening eyes of children in cars speeding by
R oman candles shooting high
K ids are sitting on dads' shoulders
S ausages sizzling at the hot-dog stand.

Craig Wilson (12)
Uppingham Community College

KALEIDOSCOPE

Nordic races young and old, live on ice and freezing cold,
Darkness falls, northern lights, one of nature's wondrous sights.
Tropic heat, hardly rains, sun-baked scorching dusty plains.
There the natives, skin of brown, seek the shade and then lie down.
In the west the Red man roams, cabins, tepees, serve as homes.
Asian folk of yellow hue, always have so much to do.
Planting rice and ploughing too,
Building huts of stout bamboo.
Black or white I just don't care, there is so much of wonder there.
Spinning, changing, full of hope,
The world is my kaleidoscope!

Adam Hartwell (12)
Uppingham Community College

A POEM ABOUT AUTUMN

Tree leaves swirling all around
Reds, yellows upon the ground

Hear the wind in the night
Awaken to see the beautiful sight

During the day the pond freezes
Whilst walking home feel the bitter breezes

It's time to wrap up nice and warm
To prepare yourself for the coming storm.

Robert Meeney (12)
Uppingham Community College

CAPITAL KALEIDOSCOPE

Canberra is in Australia
Andorra la Vella is in Andorra
Palma is in Majorca
Ireland's capital is Dublin
Tiräna is the capital of Albania
Amsterdam is the capital of the Netherlands
Lisbon is the capital of Portugal
Cairo is in Egypt
Italy's capital is Rome
The capital of the USA is Washington DC
India's capital is New Delhi
England's capital is London
So, what about it?

The world is full of places
I have never been
The world is full of people
I have never seen
The world is like a kaleidoscope of people and places.

Andrew Bryant (12)
Uppingham Community College

NO SMOKING

Send it packing,
If you don't like hacking,
You must be sad,
To smoke a fag,
A cigar,
Or a cigarette.
They are very bad,
You can make a bet,
You're going to get very ill.

You've sent it packing.
Because you don't like hacking,
You are not sad,
You don't smoke a fag,
A cigar,
Or a cigarette.
They are very bad,
You can make a bet,
You're not going to get ill.

Tom Barnes (12)
Uppingham Community College

HATE

Your smile, not nice,
Your heart, cold as ice.
Your morbid mind
And thoughts unkind,
Your malevolent soul
Like lumps of coal.
Please dispose of your unsettling gaze
And untangle your brain's tedious maze.
Your penetrating screams, piercing my skin,
Your veins are forever exploding with sin.
Your venomous sting, your deadly bite,
You will continue to fall from a very great height.

Natalie Sands (14)
William Bradford Community College

I Wish . . .

He works
He works away from home,
He goes on Mondays
He's back on Fridays.

He drives a car
A fast one too,
The way he takes the bends
And handles the car.

I don't see him very often
He's always out with his mates,
Having a drink,
Having a laugh.

He hasn't got a girlfriend
I wish he was mine,
I wish I was older
Then I'd be happy.

He's a twin
His brother is so alike to him
But I know the difference
And I know he'll always be mine.

Nicola Screaton (14)
William Bradford Community College

Dusk To Dawn

The heat's vapours rose from the glistening tarmac,
the horizon distorted and the humidity visible.
As the sun's piercing rays shone down
dark shadows formed in the passageways.

As the sun began to die
the shadows fell,
the darkness swallowing the scenery.
Slowly the transformation of lightness to dark concludes.
The life and light disappears from a town,
content with darkness.

Chris Lloyd (15)
William Bradford Community College

SOLITARY

I'm drifting, drifting in complete isolation,
Grim, grave in total desperation.
I'm thinking pessimistically,
I'm experiencing doubt, panic and anxiety.
I am beginning to get delirious
But yet I am lugubrious.
In front of me I see a huge feast,
And in the centre is a giant horned beast.
I'm holding a glass or rich red wine,
This scene I'll see again in time.
Then my head is in the water,
And a huge iron hand is pushing me under.
These are my mirages, my hallucinations,
Still miles I am from civilisation.
Here I am on the great wide ocean,
The waves are making a beckoning motion,
The easy way out would be to jump over the side,
But survival and life is what I decide.
So utterly friendless on my endless journey,
Completely and altogether solitary.

David Nettleship (15)
William Bradford Community College

STRANDED

My heart is pounding,
the noise is deafening.
Sitting in a corner
is a young girl.

She wept as she sat there alone,
no one to comfort her only a small bear.
She cried out for her mum and dad,
but nobody came.

The tears rolled down her cheeks,
she stared at me;
feeling the hurt in her heart
I picked her up and ran.

Elize Wright (14)
William Bradford Community College

THE HOLIDAY

They come to this place every year
Couples, families full of cheer
They sit out there in the blazing sun
To get a good tan, they call it fun
Sunstroke, dehydration, blisters and more
Then saddened because they've got so sore
They save all year for two weeks of laze
And it's ruined in a couple of days.

Karlie Jones (14)
William Bradford Community College

PURPLE MONKEY

Purple monkey goodness me,
Whatever shall I do.
They invited me to tea,
Then they hung me in the loo.
That was a lousy thing to do,
I should be up a tree.
Not hanging from a cistern,
In some old lavatory.
They told me that I had a smell,
I told them that's my job.
But they just said, 'Shut your face,
Or I'll feed you to the dog.'
Grandad comes in puffing pipe,
And quickly lifts the seat.
Then he stands and stares at me,
And pees all on his feet.
May comes in quiet often,
I never fail to see.
But I know what she's doing,
When she turns her back on me.
But I will get my own back,
Just you wait and see.
When they're in bed all snug and warm,
And listening to the rain,
I'll be having lots of fun swinging on the chain.
Then perhaps they will move me,
And put me by the TV
Now who's the monkey!

Sarah-Jayne Hiorns (14)
William Bradford Community College

THE TACKLE

The player had come running forward,
In possession of the ball,
I could not let him come past me,
I had to stand big and tall.

He tried to push the ball past me,
I stood up straight in his path,
Then I leapt at the ball at his feet,
It might mean a quick early bath!

Looking around I see faces,
Staring directly at me,
Angrily shouting and chanting,
No friendly faces I see.

Danny Adcock (14)
William Bradford Community College

STROKE

When I come home from gym,
I open the door and see my nanny
As still as can be.

I see her on the sofa, closed eyes and still,
Looking calm and gentle, but she had a chill.
My grandad all panicky, as you would expect.
When help comes, she still is calm,
Goes in the ambulance,
I am scared,
Affects her life forever.

Andrew McQuillan (14)
William Bradford Community College

LIFE

Through the iced sapphire water glides,
Bubbles of moon green stars.
Piercing the ocean with crisp fresh rays,
The liquid sun of fire.

Metallic sparks of fish dart,
Through the swaying beds of kelp.
As light dances through the waves,
And spills over iced caps.

As pearled water droplets fly,
Through the frosted air,
A song of life can be heard
Echoing off marine rock.

Piercing screams of radiated joy,
And squeals as freedom envelops.
In a beat of splintered glass,
A lone tail whips the salted sea.

But a new element enters the song.
The melody of an approaching trawler
Breaking the crystal waves
Of echoing harmony.

Through the mist of silver,
A steel bladed harpoon
Thirsty for life.
How will the song of life end?

Mark Short (14)
William Bradford Community College

THE SEA LION

The sea is a wild lion,
Leaping, mauling and clawing
At the sandy shores.
He lives in anger in the caves,
But when his prey comes into sight
He leaps to action,
Breaking down rock,
Crushing small ships
With his deadly jaws.

He jumps and spits, snarls and writhes
At sailors desperate to survive.
But when the wind stops blowing,
And the rain stops shooting down,

The reverse side of the cat
Comes out of the shadows,
Into the sun rays.
The gentle, timid kitten
Comes out to play.
Rolling round and purring
So quiet and still.

James Midgley (14)
William Bradford Community College

22-12-66

Where did you go
Three and a half years back?
You were misunderstood.
If you returned,
so much disorder,
what then?

You disappeared from the face.
Where are you now?
At least you belong.
Though I never knew you,
I miss you still.

Carla Mundy (14)
William Bradford Community College

SNOW AND ICE

The snowflakes began to fall from
the cold grey sky, slowly at first
and then increasing in volume until
all that could be seen was a
vast white curtain of snow.

A soft carpet of snow formed,
covering like a blanket everything
in its wake, until all that could be
seen was a white wilderness
of complete desolation.

As young children began to build
snowmen from the brilliant white
snow, small icicles began to form
from frozen droplets of water,
underneath the window ledges.

And like in our hallucinations of
him, Jack Frost began his morning
rounds, chilling us to the bone with
his ice-cold breath, as winter
clasped its icy fingers around the land.

Richard Smith (15)
William Bradford Community College

SILENT DEATH

The F117-A glided through the sky,
In the comfort that they would
Not be seen on enemy radar,
And also knowing they would not be heard.

Flying over its target, the pilot
Looked down, watching tanks and soldiers
Marching in the city.
Suddenly a red laser was seen,
Coming from the plane and pointing at
The Presidential Palace, but no one noticed.

Then the plane's bomb dropped and everyone
Noticed the first flash and then the shockwave.
The tanks and soldiers were no more.

Craig Green (15)
William Bradford Community College

THE VERT

It was scary,
Standing fifteen feet up,
I counted to three then went,
Flying down vertical,
My stomach in my mouth,
Then I hit the transition,
Then back up the other side,
The wheels on my skates were warm,
Yes, I'd done it,
The biggest vert in England.

Nathan Edwards (14)
William Bradford Community College

A PERFECT DAY

Down on the beach,
Where the sand is warm
and the stones and pebbles lay,
The waves are calm
and the ships are still
throughout the tranquil day.
The people on the beaches
with their deckchairs and their kids,
waiting in the queues for the donkeys
and all for just a quid!
The sun is bright, there is no breeze,
you could say a perfect day!

Abigail Bucknall (14)
William Bradford Community College

THE WIND

A bull
Charging through the night
Destroying homes by the hundred
In the morning
The bull goes back
To his barn in the sky.

Graham Jones (14)
William Bradford Community College

LEICESTERSHIRE

Leicestershire cricket team are the best,
With Wells and Maddy opening the batting,
Followed by Smith, Sutcliffe and Habib's half centuries.
Then Simmons, Nixon and Lewis slogging the ball around,
And Millns, Mullally and Brimson bringing up the tail end.

The marvellous bowling over the two innings wins the game,
With Mullally and Lewis, the fast bowlers, taking the opening wickets.
Wicket-keeper Nixon behind the stumps,
Lewis and Simmons in the slips catching any balls that get an edge.
Then Brimson, Millns, Simmons and Wells finishing off the tail-enders.

Happy memories of Wells' brilliant figures of 5-18,
And Millns getting the excellent score of 99,
Both in the same league game.
Getting to the final of the Benson & Hedges Cup,
When Lewis bowled a Yorker to get Adam Hollioke out
                                        in the semi-final.
The unlucky feeling of losing to Derbyshire in the Natwest semi-final.

David Cumbley (14)
William Bradford Community College

WINTER

Lamplight glowing
bar of chocolate
steaming mug of tea
curled in front of the fire
lost in my favourite book
in winter this is me.

Sian Pateman (14)
William Bradford Community College

A WALK IN AUTUMN

Leaves, falling, floating, rustling -
A crunchy carpet under my feet.
Throwing them up in the air and
running through them.
Smelling like ripe fruit.
Swithland Woods on a warm, sunny day
With a bright blue sky above.
My family enjoys walking through the woods
We laugh and joke and have a chatter.
Along the paths the trees are bony, bare
and a few pebbles are shiny and bright.
On the riverbank we enjoy watching the boats go by.

Donna Shaw (14)
William Bradford Community College

HEADACHE

Stop all the clinging and the clanging,
Stop the phone ringing and the stereo banging,
Please help me my head is hanging
On the floor, my body rattling.

Round and round the room spins,
Still I support myself with my now weak pins,
Please help me before someone sins.

Head pounding, arms wrapped round,
Please say that it's some paracetemol that I have found.

Roy Foster (14)
William Bradford Community College

THE LAST TRICK

The curtain rose,
And there she was.
A fairy of ice and snow,
Shimmering in the spotlight.
She was the ballerina of her dreams,
Dancing with her prince,
So slow, so grand.
Becoming faster and sparkling,
Leaping into the heavens.
They all joined in,
Whirling faster and faster,
Until suddenly her world disappeared.
And she was home,
Once more.
Alone with her dream.

Keelin Ryan (14)
William Bradford Community College

THE SLAVE

She hurts me,
She sends me up the shop,
But I love her.
She makes me do all kinds of things,
She makes me cook for her,
But I love my big sister Rachael.
But now it's my turn with my little sister Rhiannon.

Richard Brookes (14)
William Bradford Community College

How I Feel

I lie there crying day and night
About that man with all his might
Like a nightmare I just lay there
Wondering is anyone would really care
The humiliation of what he did
After all I was just a kid
There's still time, there's still hope
I just don't know whether I can cope
With all the shame of this silly game
That ended me in all this pain
The fight is over, he won the war
I feel like an apple without its core
My life's not complete, there's something wrong
Why did this go on so long?
I couldn't say, I felt so trapped
I must have been completely tapped
I was to blame, that's how it felt
I thought my brain was about to melt
Was I believed? I just don't know
Will this feeling ever go?
The answers are still so unclear
Of why he was found to be in the clear
I feel so hurt, I got treated like dirt
I wasn't old enough to flirt
I'm glad I got through that test of time
Like a wall I had to climb
The humiliation of what he did
After all I was just a fresh young kid.

Rachel Evans (16)
William Bradford Community College

THE STALLION DREAM

On calm mornings you may catch her.
Kicking up stones.
Stirring the pebbles with shining hooves.
But she is not alone.
Further out he watches and waits.
He neighs his discontent.
And the ocean heavens.
Ripples with muscular intent.
She tosses her mane and droplets dance.
Caught on the breeze.
When the sea is a mare, you may approach.
Dip in a toe.
But not if he sees.
For the stallion watching over her
Is not quite so tame.
And if he is disturbed
There's a storm in his mane.
With the wind in his nostrils.
A snort and a growl.
He'll gallop towards you crashing the shore.
Playing with her in the shallows.
But watch and beware.
Keep your eye on the horizon.
Remember he's out there.

Alison Warner (14)
William Bradford Community College

POEM

A big bump for 9 months,
It's finally here,
It's gone so slow,
It seems like a year.

The nursery's decorated,
Ready and waiting,
Toys all around,
I'm dreading the twingeing.

My bag's all packed,
Into hospital I go,
A boy, a girl,
Oh I don't know.

'A boy, a boy!'
My husband shouts.
I'm not in the mood,
'Don't shout too loud.'

The baby starts squealing,
Just had to watch his face,
To see all the wrinkles,
When he stops there's no trace.

Going home in the car,
Watching every move he makes,
The love I feel
Will never be replaced.

Gemma Hancock (14)
William Bradford Community College

A POEM ABOUT SUMMER

You know it's summer when the sun is bright,
making the days long and light.

You know it's summer when the grass is freshly cut,
and everybody's walking around barefoot.

You know it's summer when the barbecue's alight,
and everything's burnt in sight.

You know it's summer when everyone's having fun,
enjoying themselves soaking up the sun.

You know it's summer when the skies are clear,
and the sunset is arising near.

You know that summer has disappeared
now that autumn is here.

Sarah-Jayne Ellis (14)
William Bradford Community College

ALONE

I am lost and all alone,
there was total silence.
No one to talk to, no one was there.
There was not even a mouse,
just silence.
It was cold and damp,
I was scared and lonely.
There was nobody there,
no noise, no nothing,
I could not even hear
the sound of my own voice.

Nicola Shorter (14)
William Bradford Community College

ROLLER-COASTER

Scary feeling
What to do
Standing in line
Should I go through?

Beating heart
Knocking knees
Getting closer
'Tickets please!'

In the car
Off we go
It's not bad
This bit's slow.

Stomach churning
At the top
Over the hill
Is that big drop!

Lost my stomach
Down that bit
The loop is next
I'll have a fit!

Going round
Feeling sick
Glad that's over
It went quick.

Feeling dizzy
Petrified
Let's go again!
That was a good ride!

Amanda Finney (15)
William Bradford Community College

FOOTBALL FEVER

Football, football, football is all we hear,
With its tasteful shirts and cans of beer,
I don't need a doctor to see this disease,
But to find a cure would put my mind at ease.

With a black and white ball and men in shorts if
Us women had rights this footie would be in the courts,
The dream of a team winning 20-0,
I don't think so lads, I think you're ill.

Injected with the beer belly disease,
With a can of beer he feels his mind is at ease,
The tele's on and the chips are out,
The lads are here and I'm off out.

I don't need a doctor, nurse or a GP,
The symptoms of this fever are clear to me,
Owen, Giggs, Gazza too,
Are all members of this terrible flu!

Fay Masterman (14)
William Bradford Community College

THE MORNING WHEN

As I lay in my bed
I heard the phone ring,
My mum answered the phone.
I could not hear her voice
I heard her get up,
She came into my room,
My heart began to race,
I felt ill all of a sudden,
And she told me my grandad had died.

As my dad walked through the door,
I cried myself to sleep.
When I woke everything was disorientated.
I did not go to school that day because it hurt very much.

Jeanette Clough (15)
William Bradford Community College

He Was . . .

He was young, he was cool,
He made my mum look small,
He was tall, he was thin,
But he never looked dim.
He was healthy, he was fit,
And he was very strict.
Then one day he fell
And it was like our lives
Fell down a well.
He was angry and in pain,
He didn't feel the same.
He was dying, we're not lying
But I still loved him the same.
He was dull, he was ill,
He couldn't run or walk,
And he struggled to talk,
But my mum tried and tried
To make his last days worthwhile.
While he remembered the good times he had
As a husband and as my dad.

Hannah Smith (14)
William Bradford Community College

JUST A NORMAL DAY

I wake up to a punishing sound
I just sat up and frowned
I gave a groan
And got out of bed
Mum was sad
And Dad was mad
Again
I sat and thought of normal families
Sitting in the sun
Then I think of our one sitting in a dungeon
How I mourned to be that boy laughing in the sun
My parents say they'll work things out
But the only one that's losing out
Is the boy at the bottom of the dungeon.

Ryan Jeffs (14)
William Bradford Community College

UNTITLED

My bedroom door was ajar
I felt a dark force around me.
It was a dark figure without a face.
I could feel the cold beating of his heart,
I was forced down and was numb all over.
I was covered with fear
The figure pulled a knife
I was shaking inside, and frozen with terror.

Laura Rebecca Martin (14)
William Bradford Community College

LT COLONEL

The sky was lit up by the ammunition
as it ignited,
The bombs hit nearby as if there was an
earthquake below us
The first bomb hit hours ago when the
Jerries declared . . . .

The trenches are muddy, cold, wet, lonely
from civilisation
Gas bombs are being dropped and no one
has a gas mask
Soldiers are sleeping with a handkerchief
around their faces
We're all afraid, afraid, afraid
More bombs drop nearby and the air
becomes warmer

All soldiers are ready to murder the Jerries
More, more, more, more bombs are dropped
upon our heads
A bomb spins out of control straight at us
Kills some of us and you can feel death
all around us
Everyone wants to go over and murder them

But it was just a memory on bonfire night
As the fireworks are fired into the air.

Andrew Soden (14)
William Bradford Community College

HELL TOWER

The fires burned through the building
Engulfed in the hot clouds of smoke,
I could not see anything
I placed the wet cloth over my scorched face.
Would I live? Only God would know.
My life was before me.

I started to crawl into the unknown.
My hand was on a cold, soft object.
Then the heavens opened.
I felt sick when my face looked down,
My hand on its instant body
And then . . . !

Jonathan Wells (14)
William Bradford Community College

PET

I asked my mum why not
'Cause all she says is *no*
Why can't she say *yes, yes, yes*
But *no*, she just says *no*

All I want is a pet
I don't mind what it is
But I don't want a fish
They're too boring
I'd rather have a hairy spider than a fish.

Helen Hincks (14)
William Bradford Community College

THE SNOWMAN

I woke up this morning with a big of a dizzy head,
And then all I could think of was to get up out of bed.
I took a few paces forward and then felt like dropping dead.
I looked out of the window, it was snowing!
I opened the drawer and put on some clothes,
If I hadn't I would have probably froze.
I ran down the stairs and opened the door,
And there was a snowman so still and so sure.
I asked him his name and he said it was Fred,
I would have probably guessed as it was written on his head.
I asked him if he was cold as he had no clothes,
He replied 'Snowmen aren't meant to keep warm.'

Glyn Parnell (14)
William Bradford Community College

PEOPLE

P rivate people keep to themselves, but there is always one
    that gets on your nerves.
E very day when I wake up, I think of others who are a pain in the butt.
O f all the people, neighbours are normally the best.
P eople like neighbours though can sometimes be a pest.
L iving next door to a raving lunatic, who plays loud music
    at midnight and acts really hip.
E ach day when I go to school, I think hurry I'm out of it all.

Matthew Lawson (14)
William Bradford Community College

WHY?

The days are long,
And the nights are short.
The feelings are strong,
And you're still in my thoughts.

When will you be back?
I haven't a clue.
But all I know,
Is that I still love you.

Some nights I just sit and cry,
Searching my heart for a reason,
And asking myself 'Why?'

Why must you go?
Why can't you stay?

Forget all these questions
I love you anyway.

Holly Bourne (14)
William Bradford Community College

DREAMS

They seem so real,
You wish they would come true,
But then again they never do,
They sometimes seem confusing,
Then sometimes they're amusing,
But most dreams are unreal,
So I will never feel,
The fulfilment of my dreams.

Elizabeth Brown (14)
William Bradford Community College

A DIFFERENT WORLD

I see it upon the shelf
and wonder.
Should I pick it up?

I think of how it was made,
how many trees were used,
how many thoughts thought.

I see it looking at me,
telling me,
controlling me.
I fight back but,
I give in.

I pick it up and
look through it
page by page.

I'm in a different world,
a world of knights and dragons,
goblins and wizards.

The last page is turned,
and I enter,
reality,
once more.

Julie Killick (14)
William Bradford Community College

FOOTBALL/FUSSBALL

Football is a national game,
Football, fussball it means the same,
The joy of a goal that could win the game,
50,000 fans chanting 'Do it again!'

22 players kicking a ball,
From the centre to the box it could be a goal,
Breaths are held as the other team attacks,
A sigh of relief when the ball is won back.

The commentators cry 'What a magnificent goal!'
A roar of joy when the final whistle's blown,
Football is a national game,
Football, fussball it means the same.

Rachel Newsom (14)
William Bradford Community College

REALITY

The pounding of running feet,
The fear is spreading.
Towards danger they run,
Without even knowing.
My heart skips a beat,
As the fearful sound comes.
Then the silence
That sends me numb.

As the visions appear,
On my small screen,
Tears well in my eyes,
Are these people real?
The sirens are loud,
They ring in my ears.
How will these people live,
With the everlasting fear?

Victoria Yeomans (15)
William Bradford Community College

TRENCH WARFARE

Life in the trenches
Not the easiest thing
The crackling of gunfire
Echoing in your head.
The crunching on the tank
As it runs over the dead
Boom, boom, that one was close.
Commander screaming his orders
Drums your ear
Move out, halt, fire.
Hours later, bodies everywhere
So silent you can hear
Whispers so that's
Life in the trenches.

Adrian Yates (14)
William Bradford Community College

CAT

He prowled through the
long, long grass.
Stalking his victim through the
long, long grass.
Following it ever so carefully,
until he had it in his grasp.

With every sip of milk,
he took,
he cleaned himself so
gracefully.
Then by the fire he sat,
this is so typical
of my cat.

Christiane Bellerby (14)
William Bradford Community College

SUMMER

Spring has finally gone,
And the sun has brightly shone.
Children playing in the sun,
Having lots of fun.
Ice-creams melt,
Little boys' socks smelt.
Sausages sizzle and burgers are burnt,
My father just hasn't learnt.

Le-Anna Dewis (14)
William Bradford Community College

WAR TIME

On the battlefield,
Dressed in green.
32 leather webbing,
Heavy and dank.
An Enfield, 303 rifle
Heavy with the wet.

Here they come,
Shells explode.
Gas masks on,
It's mustard gas!
Death in the trenches
One man can't get
His gas mask on . . . dead.

He coughs up blood,
Choking, choking, choking.
4 or 5 more shells explode,
The ground sighs and bubbles,
As the breath exhales from the dead.

Now it's my turn to meet
My maker, as I scream and
Wallow in pain, I see a bright
White light.
See ya lads, that's me gone.

Jonathan A Woodward (14)
William Bradford Community College